United States
Department of
Transportation

Volpe National
Transportation
Systems Center

May 2007

I0426117

Mendenhall Glacier Visitor Center

Vehicular and Pedestrian Congestion Study

Final Report

REPORT DOCUMENTATION PAGE		Form Approved OMB No. 0704-0188

The public reporting burden for this collection of information is estimated to average 1 hour per response, including the time for reviewing instructions, searching existing data sources, gathering and maintaining the data needed, and completing and reviewing the collection of information. Send comments regarding this burden estimate or any other aspect of this collection of information, including suggestions for reducing the burden, to Department of Defense, Washington Headquarters Services, Directorate for Information Operations and Reports (0704-0188), 1215 Jefferson Davis Highway, Suite 1204, Arlington, VA 22202-4302. Respondents should be aware that notwithstanding any other provision of law, no person shall be subject to any penalty for failing to comply with a collection of information if it does not display a currently valid OMB control number.
PLEASE DO NOT RETURN YOUR FORM TO THE ABOVE ADDRESS.

1. REPORT DATE (DD-MM-YYYY) 14-05-2007	2. REPORT TYPE Final Report	3. DATES COVERED (From - To) 7/2006 - 5/2007

4. TITLE AND SUBTITLE	5a. CONTRACT NUMBER
Mendenhall Glacier Visitor Center Vehicular and Pedestrian Traffic Congestion Study: Final Report	USFS Alaska Region 061A-111(0500-120
	5b. GRANT NUMBER
	NA
	5c. PROGRAM ELEMENT NUMBER
	NA

6. AUTHOR(S)	5d. PROJECT NUMBER
Machek, Elizabeth C. Fisher, Frances B. Peirce, Sean Ritter, Gary Spiller, David	FHWA/Volpe # HW3E & USFS/Volpe # VXA9
	5e. TASK NUMBER
	5f. WORK UNIT NUMBER

7. PERFORMING ORGANIZATION NAME(S) AND ADDRESS(ES)	8. PERFORMING ORGANIZATION REPORT NUMBER
Volpe National Transportation Systems Center 55 Broadway Cambridge, MA 02142	DOT-VNTSC-USDA-07-01

9. SPONSORING/MONITORING AGENCY NAME(S) AND ADDRESS(ES)	10. SPONSOR/MONITOR'S ACRONYM(S)
United States Department of Agriculture Forest Service Alaska Region PO Box 21628, Juneau, AK 99802-1528 Federal Highway Administration - Western Federal Lands Highway Division 610 East Fifth Street, Vancouver, Washington 98661	USFS; FHLP
	11. SPONSOR/MONITOR'S REPORT NUMBER(S)

12. DISTRIBUTION/AVAILABILITY STATEMENT
Public distribution / availability

13. SUPPLEMENTARY NOTES

14. ABSTRACT

The Mendenhall Glacier Visitor Center of Tongass National Forest in Juneau, Alaska, is experiencing vehicular and pedestrian congestion. This study was initiated by the United States Forest Service, Alaska Region, in cooperation with the Western Federal Lands Highway Division of the Federal Highway Administration. The study objective was to identify feasible alternatives for alleviating vehicular and pedestrian congestion.

Safety and wayfinding improvements are recommended before the opening of the 2007 season. In the short term, traffic management strategies and minor design changes to moderate the flow of visitors are recommended and four alternatives are provided. In the long term, a more comprehensive management plan to assess and plan for resource use is recommended. Transportation considerations for that planning process are provided.

15. SUBJECT TERMS
Tour bus, motor coach, congestion, Tongass National Forest, Mendenhall Glacier

16. SECURITY CLASSIFICATION OF:			17. LIMITATION OF ABSTRACT	18. NUMBER OF PAGES	19a. NAME OF RESPONSIBLE PERSON
a. REPORT	b. ABSTRACT	c. THIS PAGE	NA	128	Gary Ritter
None	None	None			19b. TELEPHONE NUMBER (Include area code) 617-494-2716, ritter@volpe.dot.gov

Reset

Standard Form 298 (Rev. 8/98)
Prescribed by ANSI Std. Z39.18

Table of Contents

Executive Summary

The Mendenhall Glacier Visitor Center of Tongass National Forest in Juneau, Alaska, is experiencing vehicular and pedestrian congestion. This study was initiated by the United States Forest Service, Alaska Region, in cooperation with the Western Federal Lands Highway Division of the Federal Highway Administration. The study objective was to identify feasible alternatives for alleviating vehicular and pedestrian congestion with particular focus on options that would not require extensive alteration of the Visitor Center complex, pending a Mendenhall Glacier Recreation Area Management Plan that is to be developed beginning in 2007.

Existing Conditions
Mendenhall Glacier has experienced rapid growth in visitation as Juneau's popularity as a cruise-ship destination has grown, resulting in visitation peaks that in recent years have exceeded site-design capacity by 20-25%. Traffic congestion results from strong peaks in visitation on particular days at particular times and is associated with onshore bus excursions that bring cruise-ship passengers to the site. Fortunately, only moderate growth in tourism is expected over the long term, as both the City of Juneau and the cruise-ship industry view further growth in cruise-ship visitations as having largely reached its limit.

Although the vast majority of Mendenhall Glacier visitors arrive by tour bus, the capacity for bus operations at the Visitor Center is limited, and the existing circulation pattern mixes private vehicle, bus, bicycle, and pedestrian traffic. During peaks in visitation, pedestrian and vehicular congestion occurs at multiple locations. Current traffic congestion degrades the visitor experience with delays, crowding within the Visitor Center, disorientation and confusion due to insufficient information, bus noise, and tailpipe exhaust emissions. In addition, current facility design and operations involve several pedestrian-vehicular conflict points that are potential safety hazards.

Alternatives Development
Using site observations conducted during August 2006, analysis of data from past seasons, stakeholder interviews, and a survey of management practices in public lands and a forecast of tourism trends,[1] a wide-ranging set of nearly 40 strategies for alleviating congestion was developed. On the basis of these observations and input from a technical review group comprising representatives from both the Federal Highway Administration and the Federal Transit Administration, a set of four alternatives was created.

Findings and Conclusions
The Mendenhall Glacier Visitor Center site, as designed and as operated during the 2006 season, cannot comfortably accommodate current volumes of tour-bus operations without active traffic management. Variable grade, wetlands, and viewsheds limit options for adding capacity through expanded bus facilities in the immediate Visitor Center area. It

---

[1] These can be found in Appendices III and IV.

is evident that alternatives that provide additional tour-bus capacity without Visitor Center capacity improvements are likely to further degrade the visitor experience. Thus, going forward, any physical capacity expansion needs to be considered as part of an overall assessment of site visitation and utilization. The appropriateness of all but the most minor construction improvements cannot be determined until the Mendenhall Glacier Recreation Area Management Plan is completed because any lasting physical changes to the site should be made compatible with the long-term vision articulated in that plan.

In the near term, traffic congestion can be improved through three complementary actions: (1) signage and wayfinding, (2) management and staffing, and (3) reconfiguration. Each action can incorporate minor, moderate, or major changes that will result in varying degrees of improvement. To maximize benefits, some improvements should be implemented from each action area.

Safety and wayfinding improvements are recommended before the opening of the 2007 season. In the short term, traffic management strategies and minor design changes to moderate the flow of visitors are recommended. In the long term, a more comprehensive management plan to assess and plan for resource use is recommended. Transportation considerations for that planning process are provided.

1.0 Introduction

Mendenhall Glacier Visitor Center (MGVC, or the Visitor Center) of Tongass National Forest (NF) in Juneau, Alaska, is experiencing vehicular and pedestrian congestion. Current congestion levels at the Visitor Center create potentially unsafe conditions for pedestrians, degrade the visitor experience, and negatively affect the local environment. This study, conducted by the Volpe National Transportation Systems Center, was initiated by the United States Forest Service (USFS), Alaska Region, to identify feasible alternatives for alleviating vehicular and pedestrian congestion. The study was designed to complement the longer-term Mendenhall Glacier Recreation Area Management Plan, which will begin in 2007.

Visitation is not spread evenly throughout the year or even throughout the day; rather, there are strong peaks on particular days at particular times, which align with onshore bus excursions offered to cruise-ship passengers. Capacity for bus operations at the Visitor Center is limited, and the existing circulation system mixes private vehicle, bus, bicycle, taxi, and pedestrian traffic. During peaks in visitation, pedestrian and vehicular congestion occurs at sites throughout the area. Contributing factors include the overall demand on facilities with limited capacity, facility design and operations, tour-bus-driver behavior, and visitor behavior.

This report outlines existing conditions and recommends a two-pronged approach to alleviating the problem. In the short term, traffic management strategies and minor design changes to moderate the flow of visitors are recommended. In the long term, a more comprehensive management plan to assess and plan for resource use is recommended.

2.0 Methodology

In preparing this report, Volpe Center staff members:

- Performed a literature review and survey of bus management practices.

- Interviewed stakeholders from USFS, the City and Borough of Juneau, tour-bus and shuttle companies, and bus drivers.

- Reviewed data provided by the Forest Service, including visitation data and Visitor Center comment cards.

- Visited the site and documented conditions.

- Collected and analyzed data on bus drop-off and pick-up activity, parking occupancy, and pedestrian behavior. Data were collected over a four-day period during August 2006, which included peak times as identified by USFS staff.

Analysis of existing conditions, data from past seasons, and stakeholder interviews, along with a survey of management practices in public lands, were used to develop a wide-ranging set of strategies for alleviating congestion. Impacts on congestion as well as safety, visitor experience, stakeholders, and the natural environment were considered. This analysis led to the development of both short- and long-term alternatives.

Evaluation criteria were developed with the Forest Service. As the goal of this study was to identify feasible alternatives, these are presented at the conceptual level. Further planning and design work is necessary for implementation. Consequently, criteria are largely qualitative in nature and are used to evaluate impacts relative to other options.

3.0 Background

3.1 Mendenhall Glacier

More than 900,000 visitors travel to Juneau each year on cruise ships, and Mendenhall Glacier (the Glacier) is one of the most popular onshore destinations. Mendenhall Glacier Visitor Center, the first such center in the National Forest System, was built in 1962. It receives approximately 360,000 visitors each year, a number that comprises both tour groups and independent travelers. The Visitor Center was designed to accommodate 23,000 people per year. Thirty-five years after it first opened, the Visitor Center was hosting over 250,000 people per year. At that time, between 1997 and 1999, the building was renovated and enlarged to include an exhibit gallery and a theater.

3.2 Access

Visitors may reach the Visitor Center by city bus, taxi, tour bus, rental car, personal car, bicycle, or on foot (hiking). The majority of visitors arrive via tour bus, taxi, rental car, or personal vehicle. A minority of visitors take the city bus to a bus stop a mile and a half from the Visitor Center and then walk or bicycle the remaining distance. A multiuse path is available only for the first mile of the trip. Bicyclists and pedestrians must use the road shoulder for the remaining half mile.

3.3 Site and facilities

The Mendenhall Glacier site is approached via a 1.5-mile-long access road, Glacier Spur Road, maintained by the Alaska Department of Transportation. For the first mile there is a paved sidewalk, which later merges with the shoulder. The roadway culminates in a tear-shaped cul-de-sac with a grassy island, called the "teardrop" (Figure 1).

There are three parking lots. The first lot, located closest to the Visitor Center, has two universally accessible parking spaces, 15 spaces for private vehicles, and six

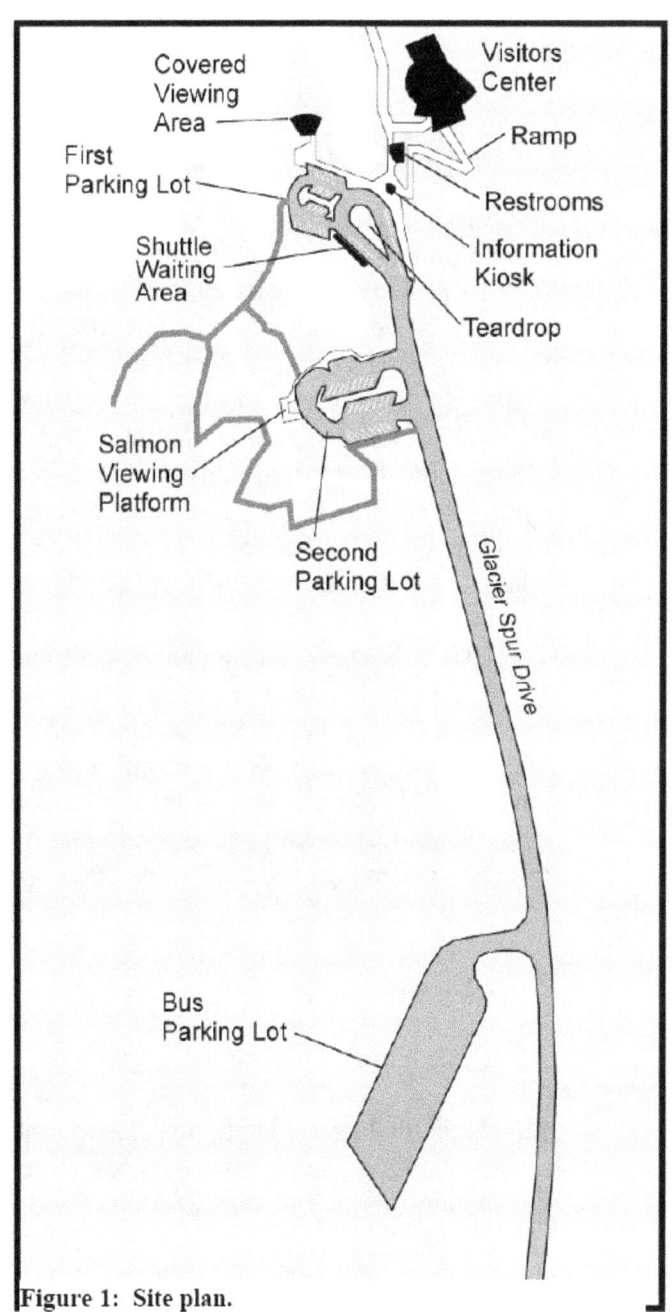

Figure 1: Site plan.

spaces for taxicabs. It is accessed off the "teardrop" turnaround area. The second parking lot is currently used for a mix of private vehicle parking and tour-bus-passenger drop-offs. It is striped to accommodate 21 RVs and 11 automobiles. Finally, a gravel parking lot (the "bus lot"), which is larger and somewhat removed from the other facilities, is provided for tour-bus-layover parking while tour patrons are visiting the Glacier.[2]

A covered viewing area provides visitors with a sheltered space to view and photograph the Glacier. An information kiosk is staffed by one or more staff members, who provide interpretation, maps, and trail information. The Visitor Center, which is located above ground level, can be accessed by an asphalt ramp, a staircase, or an elevator.

There is also a well-developed trail network, shown partially in Figure 1.

3.4 Evolution of use

The Visitor Center first opened in 1962 with a design capacity of 23,000 visitors per year. At that time, a single large paved area, located approximately where the "teardrop" and the first parking lot are today, was available for both private vehicle parking and commercial vehicle operations. In 1987, the site was redesigned to better accommodate increasing levels of bus activity; to separate pedestrian, bicycle, and vehicle activity; and to quickly orient visitors as they arrived at the site. This design created the "teardrop" and the first and second parking lots. It allowed three buses to unload on the eastern side of the teardrop so that visitors could be greeted immediately by a staff member stationed at the information kiosk. Two spaces were allocated for picking up passengers on the western side of the teardrop. The second parking lot was used as a bus parking area until what is now the bus lot was constructed in the late 1990s.

The 1987 scheme was designed to accommodate demand through levels projected to 1998. Current levels of demand outstrip this capacity and have led the Forest Service to try a variety of techniques to accommodate it. These have included active traffic management by Forest Service staff, reduced special-permit fees for tours arriving after 5 p.m., and transfer of some bus activity to the second parking lot. For the 2006 season, a new operations plan was developed in partnership with bus operators as a demonstration project. This report focuses on the 2006 operations scheme as the existing condition.

3.5 Tourism

3.5.1. Background and current conditions

Mendenhall Glacier visitation is closely linked to the development of the tourism industry in Juneau. Over the past two decades, Juneau has become an increasingly popular destination for the cruise-ship industry and has experienced rapid growth in visitation.

---

[2] The "bus lot" is not strictly reserved for use by buses. Model airplane enthusiasts and bicycle tours also make use of the space.

Approximately 950,000 tourists visited the city in 2006,[3] up from 700,000 in 1999, 480,000 during the 1994 summer season, and 240,000 during 1990[4] (Figure 2). Juneau's visitation is based largely on cruise-ship calls, which take place during the May-to-September season and are most frequent from June to August. During the 2006 season, a total of 37 vessels made 613 calls to Juneau.[5]

Cruise Ship Visitors to Juneau

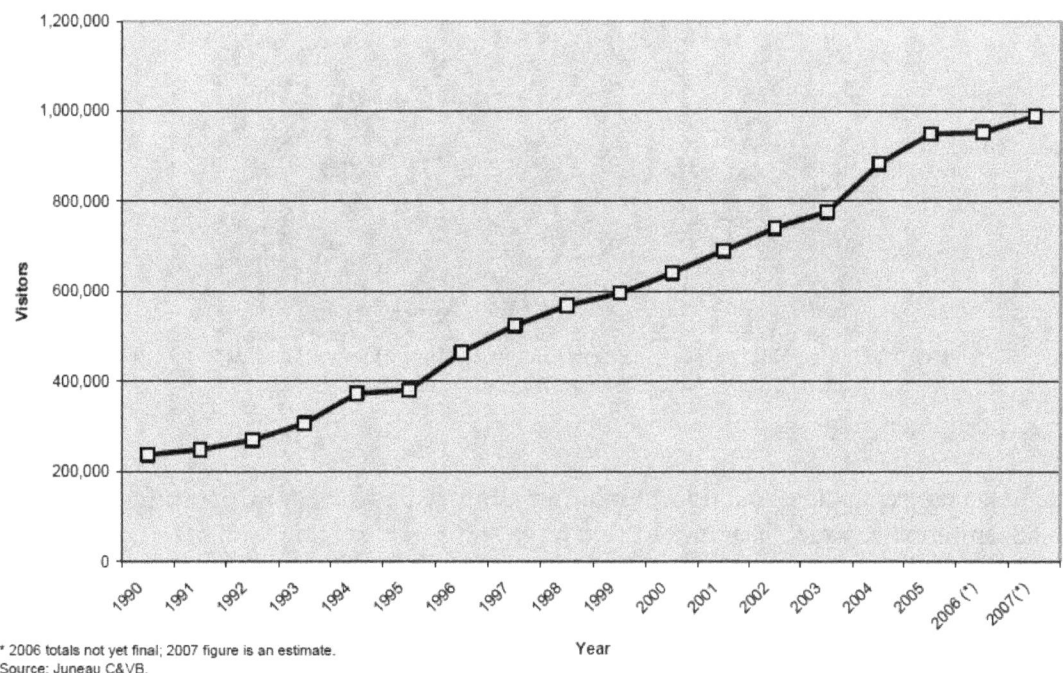

* 2006 totals not yet final; 2007 figure is an estimate.
Source: Juneau C&VB.

Figure 2: Growth in cruise ship visitation to Juneau.

While cruise passengers account for the bulk of visitors—about 85% according to the Juneau Tourism Management Plan—there are also substantial numbers of independent travelers, visitors not arriving on cruise ships. The Juneau Convention and Visitors Bureau's (C&VB) estimate for 2006 was that about 72,000 nonlocal visitors would arrive by air in Juneau. Small numbers of visitors also arrive via the Alaska Marine Highway System, private ferries, and their own vessels.

Surveys of visitors indicate that the most common activities in the area are downtown shopping and tours on the ice fields of Tongass National Forest. In the 2006 season, about 96,000 people took helicopter-based guided tours of the ice fields, often in conjunction with activities such as glacier trekking or hiking. Other popular activities include wildlife viewing; outdoor sports such as hiking, boating, and skiing; fishing; and visits to cultural and historical sites such as the Alaska State Museum. Other major

---

[3] Juneau Convention and Visitors Bureau (C&VB).
[4] City and Borough of Juneau, Juneau Tourism Management Plan (JTMP), 2002.
[5] Juneau Convention and Visitors Bureau (C&VB), Media Resource Center fact sheets.

attractions in the area are the Sawyer Glaciers, the Glacier Bay National Park, and the Inside Passage.

Figure 3: Cruise-ship passengers boarding excursion buses at the Port of Juneau.

3.5.2. Long-term outlook

Juneau is nearing the maximum level of cruise-ship visitation that its port infrastructure can accommodate, which is a limit of five large ships in port at one time: four at downtown berths and one in the harbor that is accessible via tenders. Interviews with local stakeholders indicated that this capacity constraint was unlikely to change. Even with the potential addition of a fifth berth, an option being considered by the City and Borough of Juneau to allow direct access for all five ships, there are no plans to increase the overall limit of five large ships at one time. Similarly, there are no indications that cruise lines intend to extend their season into April or October. Therefore, growth in cruise-based visitation will be limited primarily to modest increases due to the use of larger vessels. For 2006, the C&VB projected a 1% increase over 2005 levels; for 2007, it estimates an increase of approximately 4% over 2006 levels.

The development of design and management alternatives for mitigating congestion at Mendenhall Glacier assumes modest increases in tourism along these lines for the next five to ten years. Over the longer term, there is a possibility that the much-discussed Juneau Access Road, were it to be built, would connect Juneau to the continental road system and open up the area to a substantially higher level of independent tourism. This would have ramifications for the overall management of the Mendenhall Glacier site, and the change in visitor travel modes (more cars and RVs) would have implications for traffic flow around the site and the allocation of parking and loading space. Longer-term options for parking and circulation around the site will reflect this possibility as well as other longer-term changes that could influence visitation.

4.0 Existing Conditions

This section outlines the transportation operations in place at Mendenhall Glacier for the 2006 season, including buses, taxis, and private vehicles. Data were collected during both weekend and weekday periods in August 2006, with an emphasis on times identified as demand peaks by Forest Service staff. Variables observed included passenger loads, dwell times, and "straggler" behavior in addition to parking occupancy and nonmotorized travel. These variables were chosen for further study to round out detailed data on daily and hourly arrivals for the 2005 season as provided by the Forest Service. Dwell time, or the overall time a vehicle spends in the loading or unloading area, is critical to understanding current operations and opportunities for improvement.

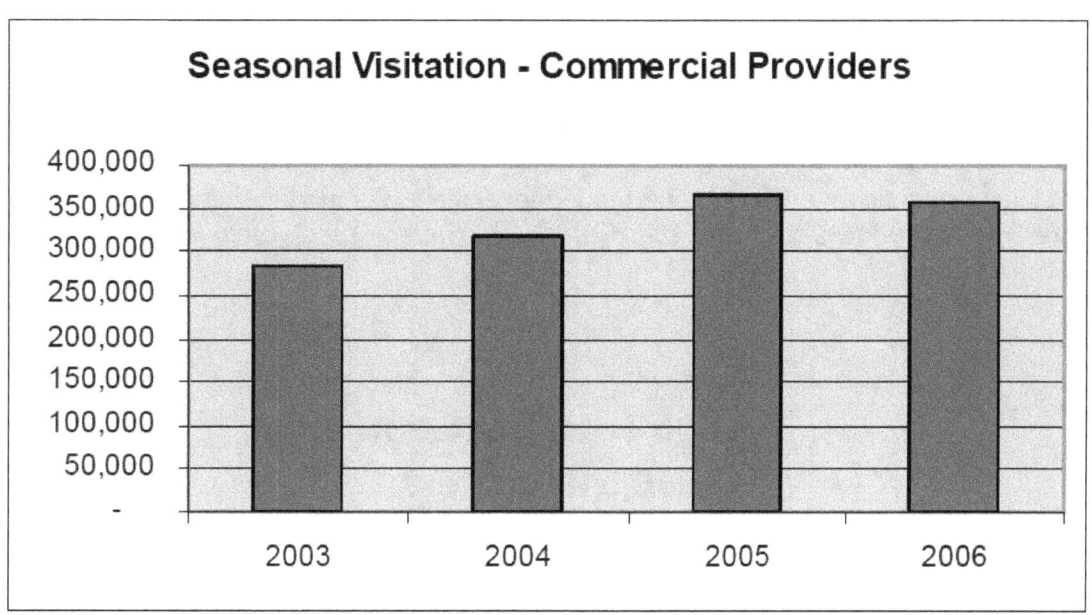

Figure 4: Number of visitors arriving by commercial transportation.

Commercial vehicle access to the Glacier is regulated through special permits, the majority of which are issued annually, with operational stipulations. The Forest Service has the ability to suspend or revoke permits for noncompliance with the terms of the permit.

4.1 Bus operations

4.1.1. Service providers

Service providers can be divided into three primary categories: "Big 3" tour operators, independent-tour operators, and shuttle services. These categories are used to present data later in this section. The pie chart in Figure 5 shows the market share that each type represents and includes taxi service as well. A description of each category of service provider follows.

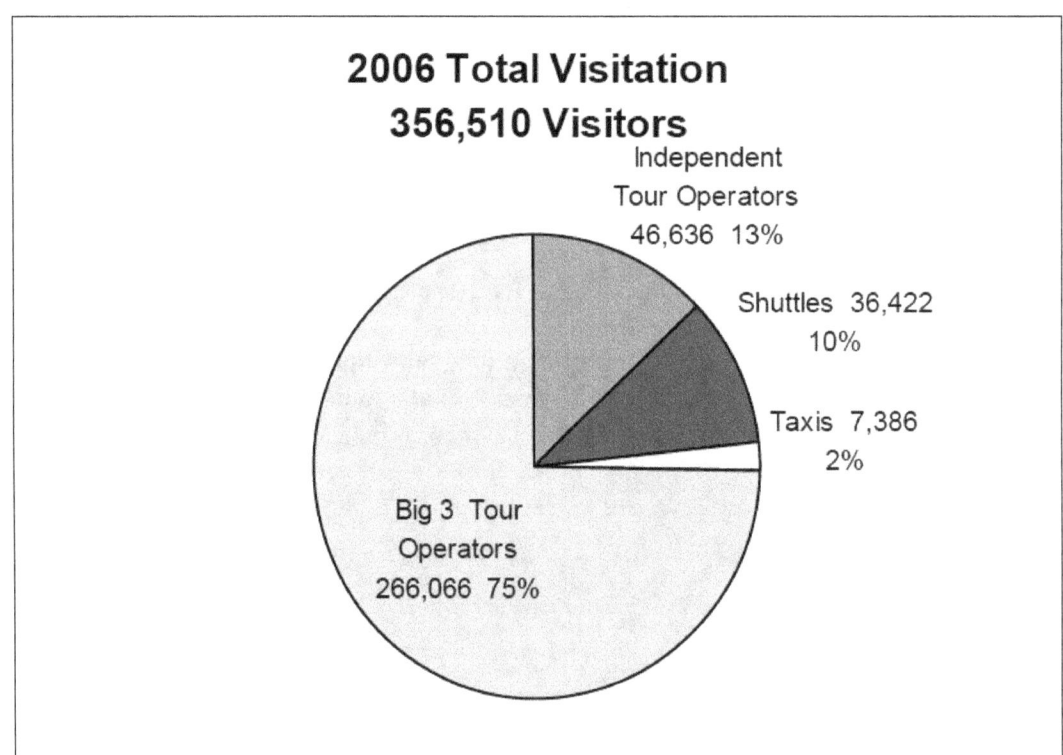

Figure 5: 2006 season commercial visitation.

The "Big 3"

The majority of tour-bus trips are conducted by three large companies, known as the "Big 3":

- Gray Line, affiliated with Holland America
- Princess, affiliated with Princess Cruises
- Alaska Coach Tours, which contracts with a variety of other cruise lines, including Norwegian

Each of these companies is affiliated with specific cruise-ship companies. Tourists who book excursions to Mendenhall Glacier through their cruise-ship company will be transported by one of the "Big 3."

The "Big 3" operate large fleets primarily composed of full-size motor coaches, although smaller buses and passenger vans are included as well.

Independent-Tour Operators and Shuttle Buses

Independent-tour operators serve cruise-ship passengers who do not prebook their shore excursions through the cruise-ship company as well as "independent travelers" who arrive in Juneau by plane or ferry. These companies are generally smaller in size than the "Big 3" and include Gastineau Guides, Last Frontier Tours, MGT, and Juneau Tours. They are not affiliated with cruise lines and sell excursion tickets onshore. Several companies offer both tour- and shuttle-bus service.

Shuttle buses provide "no-frills" transportation between the cruise-ship docks in downtown Juneau and the Glacier, running on fairly regular schedules. Both tour-bus and shuttle operators drive a mix of vehicles that includes vans, school buses, and old transit vehicles.

Cruise West

Cruise West operates smaller ships than are typically seen in Juneau and also has its own bus service. Its passengers usually come later at night, after most of the other visitors have left, and do not significantly affect operations. Smaller vehicles and the shuttle-bus area are used for Cruise West operations. Since Cruise West does not operate during peak times, its operations are not discussed in depth here.

Note on the Data

One independent company that provides small guided tours significantly affects the characteristics of independent-tour pick-ups. This company drops passengers off in the bus parking area and picks them up in the same space as do the other independent tours. Their vehicles have smaller capacities than those of other operators. In two of the five data points for this company (and in unrecorded observations), drivers arrived significantly before passengers were ready to board and then took longer for passengers to board than did most other tour services. Where this company causes significant variation in the data, information is shown for independent-tour operators with and without the company's pick-ups. Where there is great variation, the "Big 3" will be compared with independent operators without including the outlying company.

4.1.2. Pick-up and drop-off processes

Understanding the mechanics of the drop-off and pick-up processes is necessary for understanding operational issues and evaluating alternatives. During the 2006 season, three locations were used for tour-bus operations: the bus lot (for laying over), the second parking lot (for "Big 3" drop-off), and both sides of the teardrop (the east side for "Big 3" pick-up and the west side for independent-tour and shuttle operations) (Figure 6). The bus parking lot was used for laying over between pick-up and drop-off.

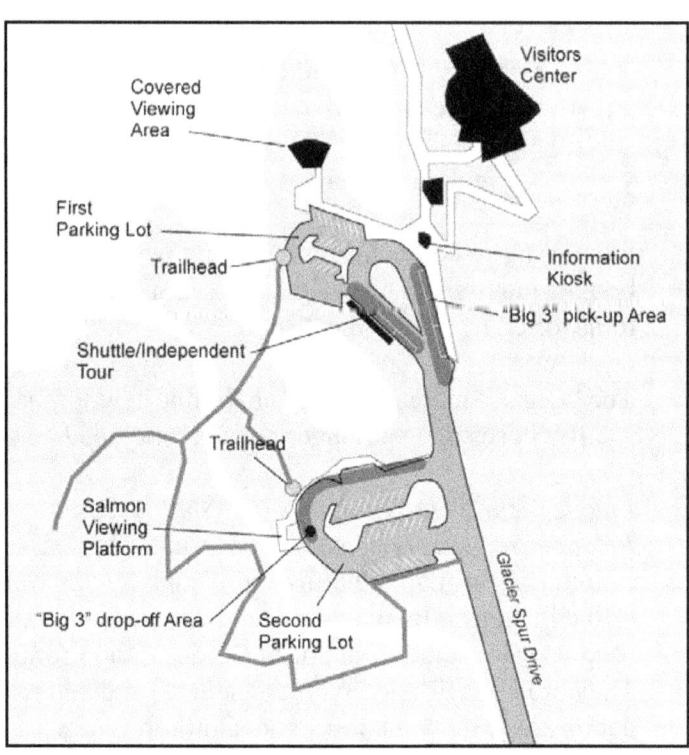

Figure 6: Visitor Center bus pick-up and drop-off areas.

"Big 3" Operations
Space is allocated for four or five "Big 3" buses to drop passengers off in the second parking lot. During observation periods, the maximum number of buses seen dropping off at a given time was five, with one bus waiting in the roadway. Drivers verbally orient passengers, providing information about access to the Visitor Center, pick-up time, and pick-up location. Passengers without mobility constraints are urged to begin their visit by way of Steep Creek Trail. For passengers with mobility constraints, drivers either tell them to use the sidewalks or drop them off by the information kiosk. This decision was made by individual drivers. After off-loading all passengers, drivers proceed to the bus parking lot to lay over until pick-up time, generally 50 minutes to one hour and 15 minutes after arrival. The length of stay is determined by the particular tour package; visits preceding activities with tight time constraints, such as whale watching or flight-seeing, are closely regulated.

"Big 3" passengers proceed to the pick-up area adjacent to the information kiosk at their designated boarding time. Space is allocated for three buses to board passengers simultaneously. The distinction between the formal boarding area and the queuing area is not well defined, and up to five buses were observed to be boarding simultaneously. As the first buses finish boarding, drivers behind them halt boarding and pull up before restarting boarding. In this fashion, boarding may take place in two or three increments.

A maximum of seven "Big 3" vehicles were observed either boarding or waiting to pick up passengers during the data-collection period. Reports from MGVC staff mentioned that the line could extend to 10 or more vehicles, with one staff member counting 17 vehicles queued at one point during the 2005 season.

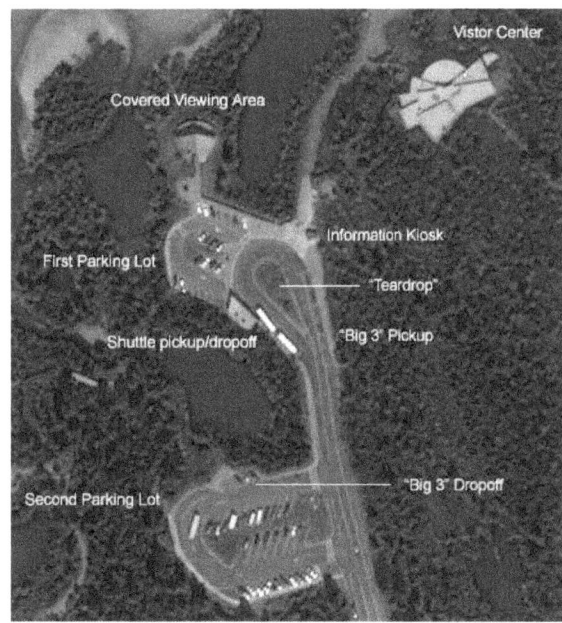

Figure 7: Aerial view of upper Visitor Center area.

Shuttles and independent-tour operations
Shuttle and independent-tour operators must drive around the teardrop to reach their assigned pick-up and drop-off area on the western side. Two spaces are allocated in this area. Independent-tour operations are similar to "Big 3" operations in that they drop passengers off, assigning a return time; proceed to the bus lot to lay over; and return at the prearranged time. Shuttle-bus operations are more streamlined; drivers proceed to the drop-off/pick-up area, off-load passengers, and then immediately board waiting passengers before leaving the Glacier area.

4.1.3. Passenger loads

Passenger loads were fairly similar for the "Big 3" and independent-tour operators. Shuttles generally had fewer passengers. Since tours are prebooked, the number of passengers is known and an operator can match an appropriately sized vehicle from its fleet to the tour size. Since shuttles are unreserved, operators generally rely on their larger vehicles to provide as much capacity as possible; still, they are limited by the fleet that they own. Table 1 shows the median, minimum, and maximum passenger loads for the three types of service providers. Smaller vehicles were often but not always used for trips with fewer passengers.

Table 1: Passenger load for the three types of service providers

Passenger Load	"Big 3"	Independent	Shuttle
Median	39	28	17
Minimum	4	3	4
Maximum	55	52	40
Data points	*92*	*92*	*35*

Figure 8 shows the number of observed vehicles with a given number of passengers for each service provider. The "Big 3" provided the majority of the trips with 20 or more passengers.

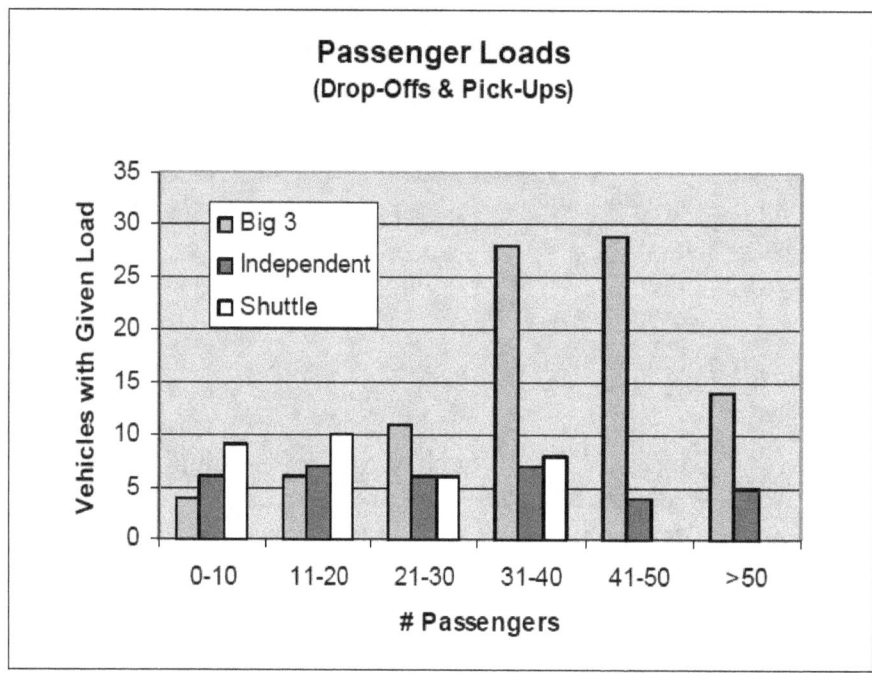

Figure 8: Passenger loads.

4.1.4. Dwell time

In this context, dwell time can be understood as the total time between arriving in the loading or unloading area and departing. It measures the amount of time necessary for picking up and dropping off passengers. It is important to understand the typical time required for drop-off and pick-up activity, as well as the range of times required, in order to determine the appropriate amount of space that should be allocated to each activity. Extreme circumstances can cause congestion during peak periods if schedules or operating concepts are designed around average operating characteristics. Five minutes for dropping off and five minutes for picking up are allowed by the operators, although this is often insufficient, especially for picking up passengers.

Drop-off dwell time
Total dwell times for dropping off passengers are shown in Figure 9.

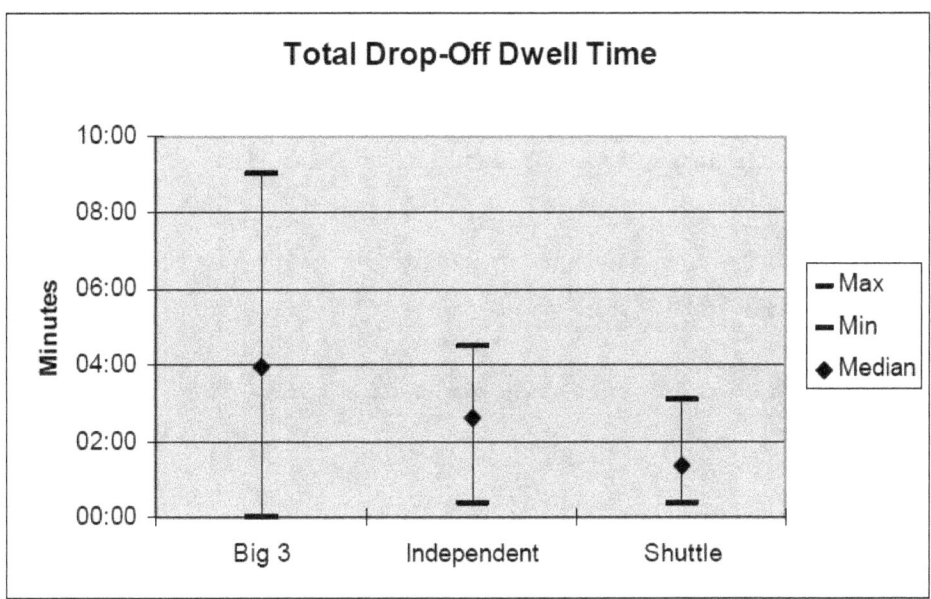

Figure 9: Drop-off dwell times.

Overall, the "Big 3" companies take longer to drop off passengers than either shuttles or independent tours. The passenger drop-off process can be broken down into three components: arrival to first passenger egress, passenger egress, and last passenger egress to departure. For each of these components, the "Big 3" companies were observed to take longer. It should be remembered that the observation period was limited and the differences in time were relatively small. Possible explanations include:

- More detailed passenger orientation was provided before passengers began to off-load.

- There was less pressure from other vehicles as the "Big 3" used a separate area for off-loading.

- Differences in passenger profiles: use of walking aids such as canes, walkers, and wheelchairs was more prevalent in the "Big 3" customer base, and removal of wheelchairs and walkers from beneath the bus added significantly to the time it took passengers to alight.

- There were more passengers on board than on other vehicle types.

Note that "egress to pull-out" data were not collected for shuttles, as after passengers off-load a new boarding cycle begins immediately.

Figure 10 shows the median time that elapsed between each component of the dropping-off process for the "Big 3," independent-tour operators, and shuttle buses.

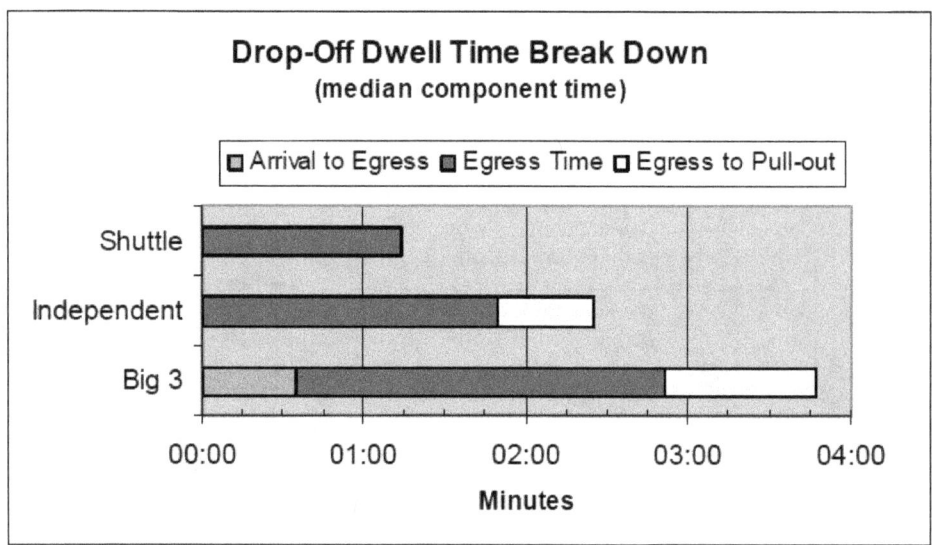

Figure 10: Drop-off dwell-time components.

Pick-up dwell time

Total dwell times for picking up passengers are shown in Figure 11. While the "Big 3" required more time to pick up passengers (7 compared with 6.5 minutes for most independent-tour operators), it should be noted that they were more efficient on a per-passenger basis (14 compared with 20 seconds per passenger for independent-tour operators). Figure 11 breaks down independent-tour operations in two ways: for all operators including the "outlier" company, and without the "outlier" company (see page 9).

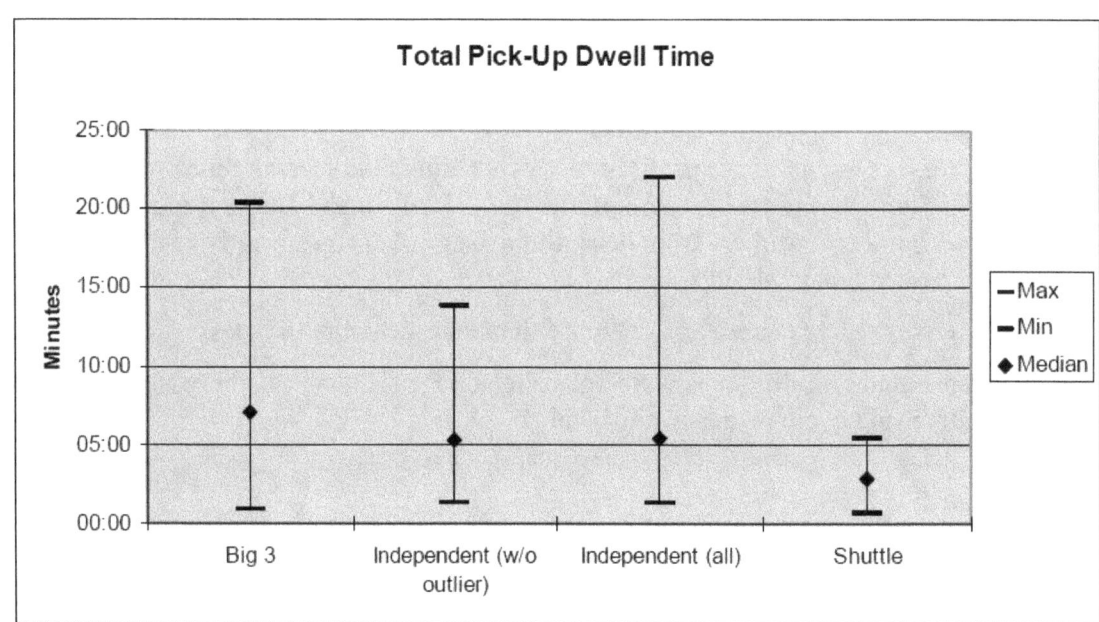

Figure 11: Pick-up dwell time.

The passenger pick-up process can be broken down into four components: arrival to first passenger boarding, queued passenger boarding, a period of waiting for "stragglers" (passengers not present in the pick-up area at the prearranged time), and boarding of the last passenger prior to departure. An overview of these components appears in Figure 12.

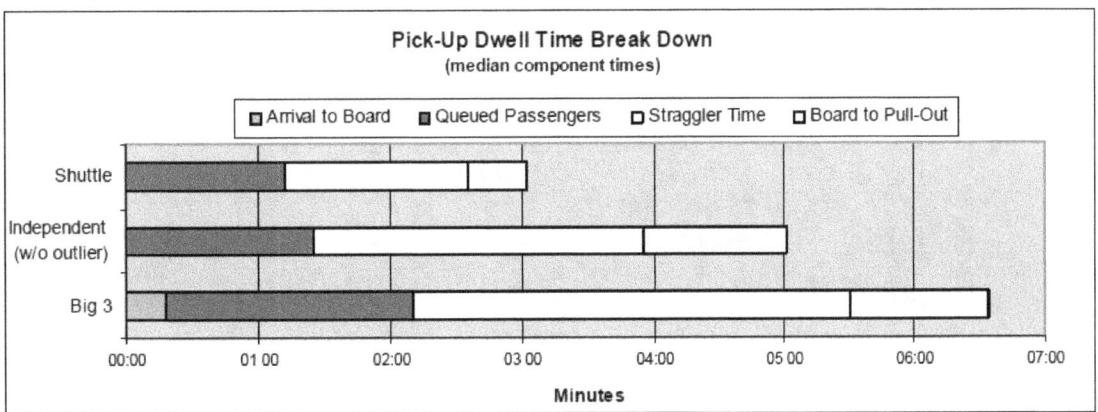

Figure 12: Pick-up dwell-time components.

Arrival time to boarding of first queued passenger: The lag observed here is likely due to the fact that the "Big 3" often allow passengers to board at unofficial spaces located beyond the end of the sidewalk. Identifying one's vehicle and then walking to these distant areas increases the time between vehicle arrival and the beginning of boarding.

Queued passengers and "stragglers": Passengers were generally waiting when their vehicle arrived. Once the vehicle was identified, passengers queued up to board. All passengers who lined up to board the vehicle when it first arrived were considered queued passengers. Passengers not in the queue were considered "stragglers."

In several instances, a bus pulled up from its initial loading position to an empty space in front. Drivers generally stopped queued passengers from boarding and directed them to board at the new location. In these instances, the count of queued passengers captured only those who boarded at the initial loading location.

For each run, both "Big 3" and independent tours have a tour group, and generally all members of each tour must return to the bus before it departs. This increases the "straggler waiting time" vis-à-vis shuttle buses, which will depart as soon as all likely passengers have boarded. "Big 3" operators generally have a policy of waiting 10 minutes (five minutes beyond the five-minute boarding window) for tardy passengers before radioing a supervisor for permission to leave them behind. In general, there was a positive but weak correlation between the total dwell time and the number of stragglers. As seen in Figure 13, even a few "stragglers" can cause a long dwell time.

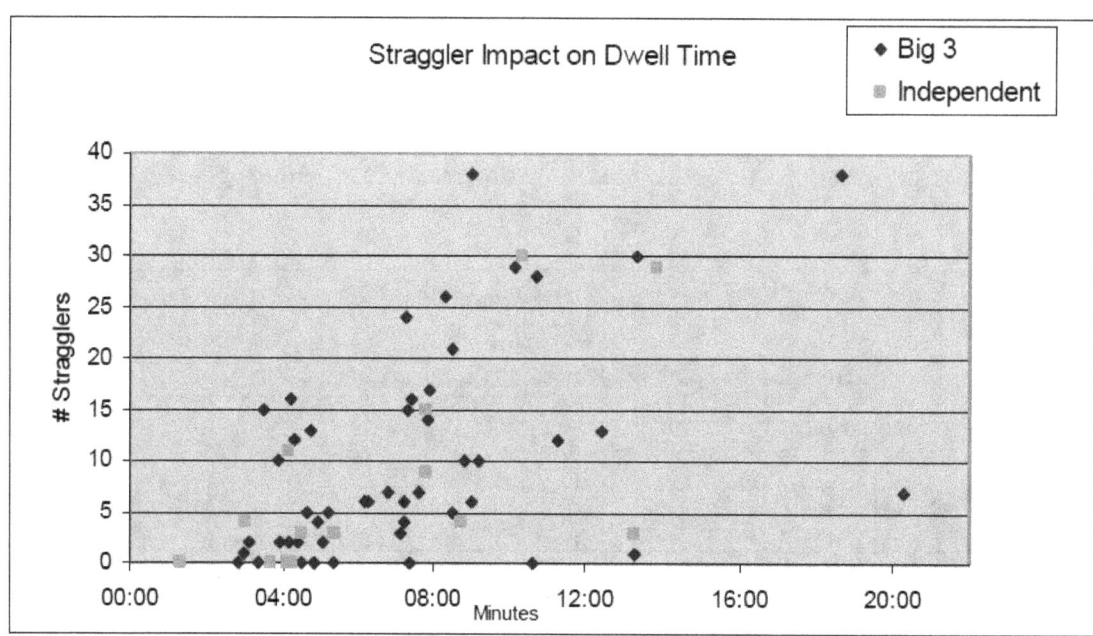

Figure 13: Total dwell time and number of "stragglers."

Departure delays: Between the times of boarding the final passenger and departing the boarding area, several conditions may cause delay. Tour-bus drivers generally performed a final headcount before pulling out. Some departure delays appeared to be related to passengers asking questions of the driver. Some vehicles were unable to leave the boarding area because they were too close to the vehicle in front and unable to back up. Several "Big 3" vehicles were able to pull away from the curb but were then stuck between the "Big 3" boarding area and the shuttle pick-up/drop-off area. This occurred because there were too many shuttle buses at the pick-up/drop-off spaces and the extra vehicles were blocking the roadway.

4.2 Taxi operations

Throughout the peak season, six spaces in the first parking lot are reserved for taxicabs. Like shuttles, taxis serve both cruise-ship passengers who do not prebook their shore excursions through the cruise-ship company and independent travelers in Juneau. Taxis offer small-group tours; typically, they pull into one of the six designated spaces in the first parking lot, lay over there until their passengers have toured the Glacier, and then depart.

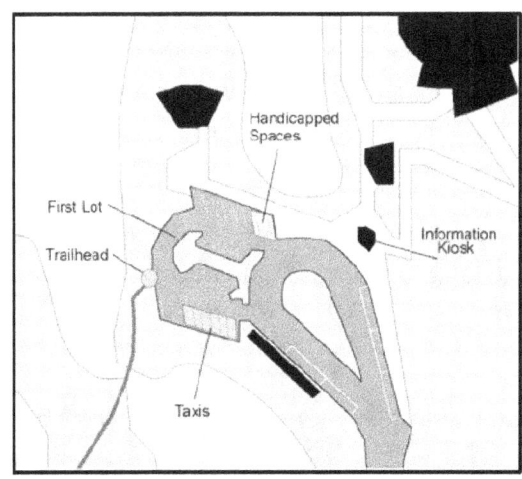

Figure 14: First parking lot.

Taxi operations were observed by assessing the usage of the six parking spaces during four periods of one to three hours during August 2006. While these data complement the qualitative information gathered from Forest Service staff, they are limited in scope and serve only as rough indicators of usage. Occupancy refers to the percentage of spaces in a given geographic area that are occupied by vehicles, either at a particular point in time or averaged across a longer time period. It is a way of measuring the intensity of parking usage and the availability of spaces.

Use of the taxi spaces corresponds roughly with the overall activity patterns at the Glacier. During the observation period, the taxi spaces were observed to be 42% occupied on average. Figure 14 shows occupancy levels recorded for each observation.

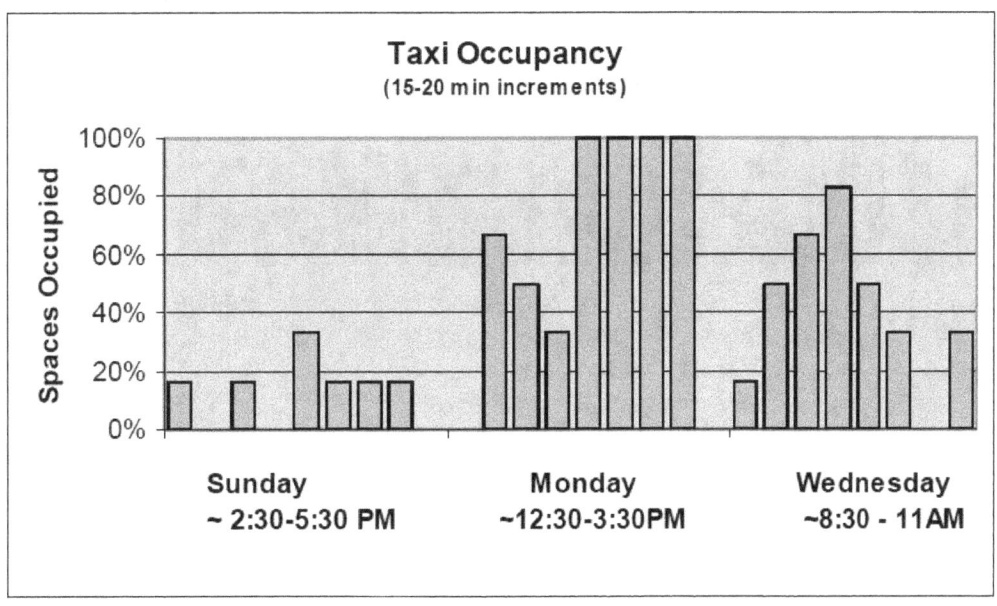

Figure 15: Taxi parking usage.

4.3 Private vehicle parking

Private vehicle parking is formally provided in the first and second parking lots. Universally accessible parking spots are provided in the first lot, and the center spaces in the second lot are striped for use by RVs. Understanding the demand for and usage of these parking spaces will inform the development and evaluation of alternatives.

Interviews with Forest Service staff indicate that, while the parking lots do fill during periods of good weather and during special events, there is a large shoulder along the road that is sufficient to accommodate demand during these infrequent peaks. Use of the shoulder for personal vehicle parking does not generally affect tour-bus operations.

Again, it should be noted that, while these data complement the qualitative information gathered from Forest Service staff, they are limited in scope and serve only as rough indicators of usage.

4.3.1. Occupancy

Private vehicle parking spaces were observed to be 79% occupied, on average, over all observations. The highest occupancy (for all private vehicle spaces) observed was 92%, although the first parking lot reached 100% occupancy during one observation.

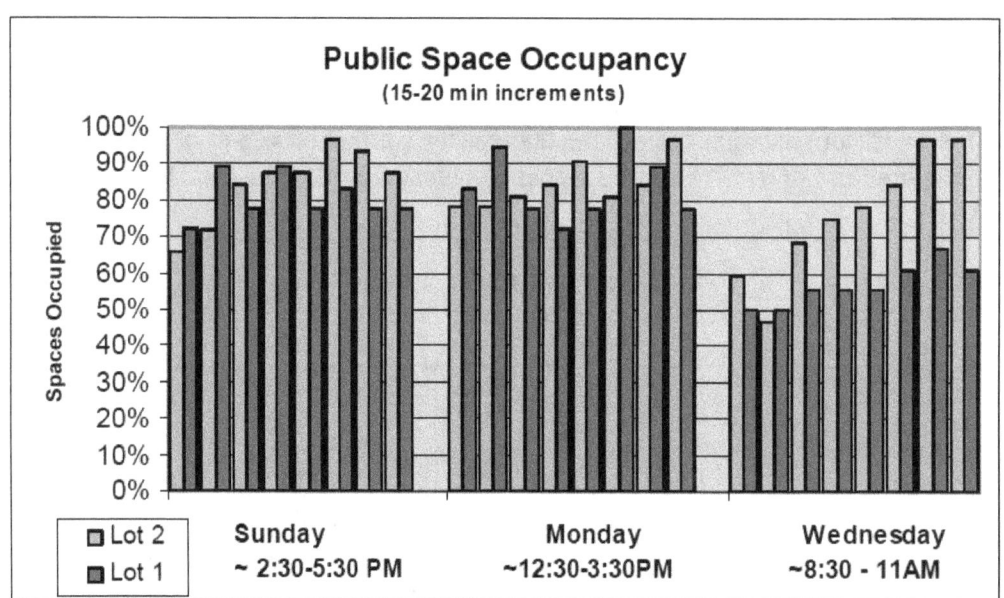

Figure 16: Private vehicle parking occupancy.

There is some additional capacity in the second parking lot in that the 21 spaces striped for RVs are large enough for two automobiles to park tandem in each spot. It should be noted that these observations counted each of these tandem spots as a single spot. Only two RVs were seen during the observation periods, suggesting that these spaces may be reduced or relocated without serious impacts.

4.4 Nonmotorized Travel

A small number of visitors were noted walking, jogging, or biking into the Mendenhall Glacier Visitor Center area. Alternative access modes were observed for two one-hour periods, a Sunday afternoon and a Wednesday morning, on Glacier Spur Road at the bus parking lot. There was a light drizzle during both periods. It is understood that more local visitors arrive, both on foot and by car, during good weather.

The majority of visitors observed were engaged in recreation or exercise: jogging, cycling, walking dogs, or hiking. Most had originally accessed the area via private vehicle. However, three groups (one consisting of two people and two, of one person each) walked from the public bus station to the Visitor Center. Two of the groups were tourists and the third was a woman working in Juneau for the summer.

5.0 Congestion

At Mendenhall Glacier, congestion is problematic inasmuch as it creates delay; it increases the potential for pedestrian-vehicle conflicts, exacerbates noise and emissions from idling buses, and otherwise negatively affects the visitor experience.

5.1 Where congestion occurs

5.1.1. Vehicular congestion

Vehicular congestion is concentrated at the wide end of the "teardrop," where it affects "Big 3" pick-ups, private vehicle and taxi access to the first parking lot, and shuttle and independent-tour-bus operations. There are occasional episodes of high congestion at the entrance to the second parking lot as well. Congestion is not an issue on Glacier Spur Road.

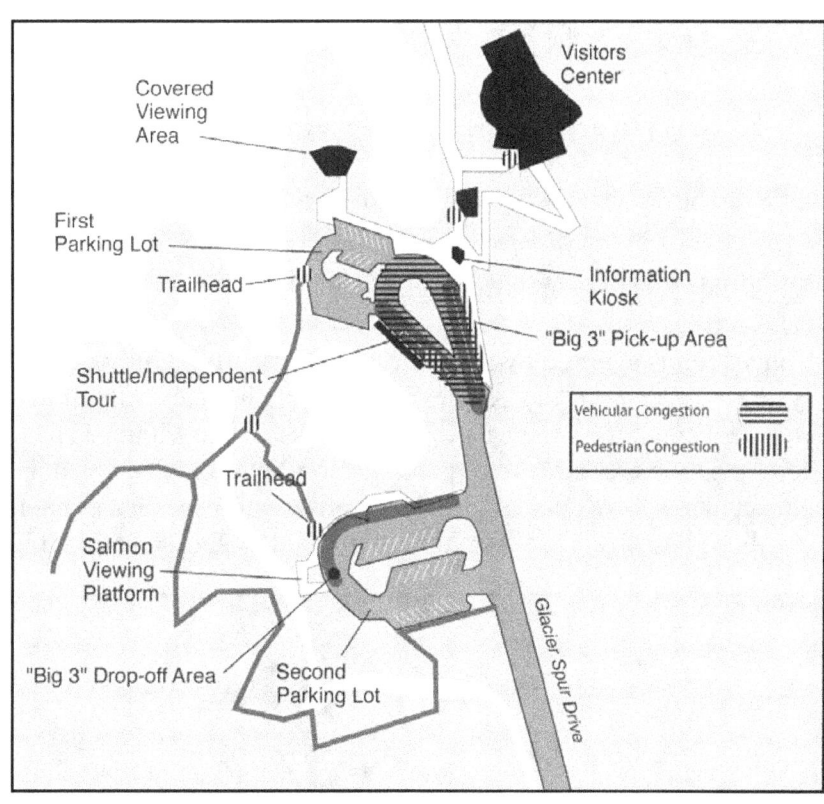

Figure 17: Congested areas.

5.1.2. Pedestrian congestion

Pedestrian congestion is driven largely by overall volumes but is also created when adverse weather conditions drive visitors to seek shelter under covered areas. Locations that experience pedestrian congestion include:

- **The sidewalk by the shuttle-bus boarding area.** Visitors walking up from the second parking lot on the sidewalk conflict with those boarding the shuttle buses. Since this path is to be used by those in wheelchairs or with other mobility constraints, the location is of concern.

- **The entrance to Steep Creek Trail.** Passengers alighting from shuttle buses tend to congregate here before entering the trail. However, some visitors linger on the trail, which has the salutary effect of spacing out arrivals and reducing congestion at the Visitor Center itself.

- **The stairway leading from Steep Creek Trail to the first parking lot.** This stairway is only three feet wide, allowing no more than two pedestrians to walk abreast. Many showed a preference for walking single file on the stairway. Since it is a two-way stairway, some visitors waited at the top or bottom for others to pass.

- **The Visitor Center entrance.** As noted above, both prepaid and nonprepaid visitors use the same entrance. At peak times, this creates congestion as staff attempt to check wristbands and direct visitors to the payment area as appropriate. Queues for the bookstore and auditorium also contribute to congestion at the entrance.

- **Covered areas.** The covered viewing area, shuttle waiting area, "Big 3" pick-up tent, and Visitor Center are all more highly used in periods of adverse weather. The Visitor Center and the tent are particularly prone to overcrowding.

5.1.3. Pedestrian-vehicle conflict

Congestion is affected by and exacerbates underlying problems with the circulation system. Pedestrian "desire lines" do not match the existing trail and sidewalk network and frequently cross the path of buses, as shown in Figure 18. Consequently, the current configuration creates several potential conflict points between pedestrians and vehicles. No accidents have been reported, and observations indicate that many visitors do in fact use the sidewalks. However, the safety of all visitors is of the highest priority.

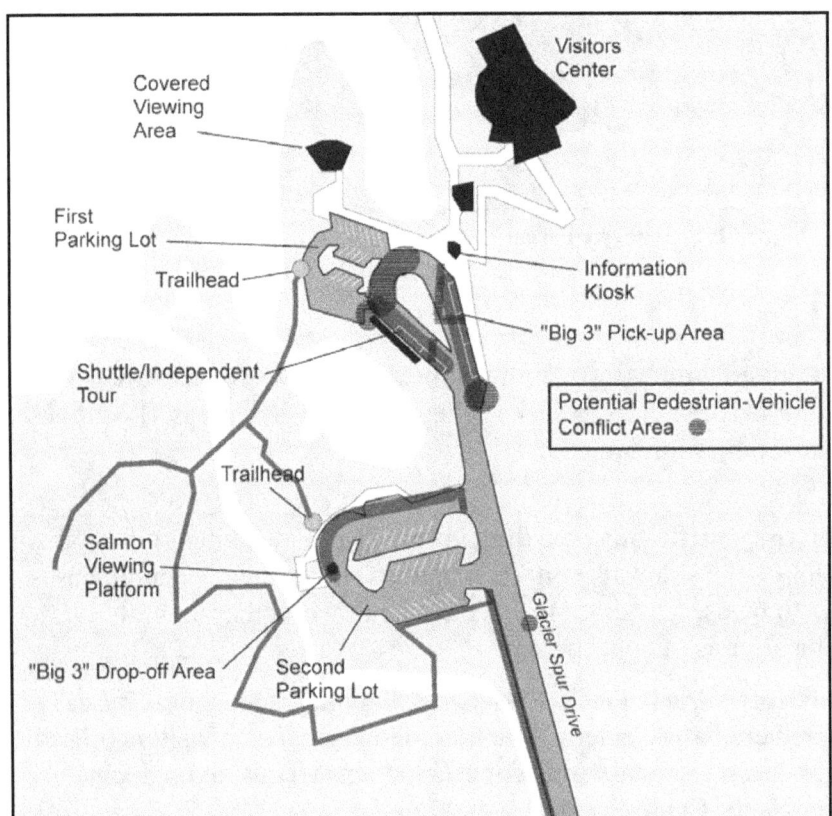

Figure 18: Potential areas of pedestrian-vehicle conflict.

Factors creating potential pedestrian-vehicle conflicts:

- Many visitors like to take photographs while posing at the Mendenhall Glacier sign on the teardrop. To reach it, they often walk in front of and behind buses and in the travel lane.

- Using the sidewalk network to reach the main facilities from the second parking lot is circuitous; many visitors prefer to cross from the second parking lot and proceed across the teardrop, directly to the main area. Again, this causes them to walk in the bus areas and the travel lane.

Figure 19: Visitors taking photos in front of the "Welcome" sign.

- It is difficult for "Big 3" passengers who are waiting to board to locate their bus from the location of the designated waiting area. They often walk out in front of buses to look down the queue. Similarly, passengers may weave around buses to board outside of the official boarding area.

- There is no sidewalk on the west side of Glacier Spur Road, and many pedestrians walk on the shoulder.

5.2 Impacts on the visitor experience

5.2.1. Passenger information

Passengers were observed waiting in the wrong area, boarding the wrong buses, being late in meeting their bus, being left behind by their bus, and being visibly distressed that they had missed or would miss their bus.

It was noted that some passengers on both the public tours and the shuttle services were anxious about the possibility of missing their bus. Most of these passengers arrived early at the pick-up location and became nervous when they did not see their bus. Their concern may be exacerbated by the lack of written information about their bus and the potential consequences of missing it, including the cost of getting back to downtown Juneau or their ship and/or missing their next activity.

Several factors contribute to passenger confusion in returning to their bus or shuttle after being dropped off:

- Having three separate areas of bus activity makes it difficult for passengers to visually locate their correct pick-up area.

- Signage is minimal and open to misinterpretation; for example, a sign by the shuttle-bus pick-up and drop-off area indicates that it is a bus zone. There is no schedule information available.

- Passengers may see their bus in the queue but be uncertain whether or not it is actively loading or queuing.

- Some buses are not labeled clearly with the company name or information on whether it is a "tour" or a "shuttle" vehicle, which increases delay associated with passengers boarding the wrong bus.

5.2.2. Delay

Cruise-ship passengers are generally tightly scheduled. Delays in pick-up and drop-off translate into less time spent exploring the Glacier area and could prevent passengers from reaching their next destination in time to participate in the activity (whale watching, etc.). It should be noted that the tour operators strive to meet their schedules, and it is likely that passengers will sacrifice time at the Glacier in order to arrive at their stop on time.

5.2.3. Noise and emissions

As drivers are queuing, many fail to shut off their engines as required by the terms of their special permits. They may also idle their engines during the boarding process. This is partially explained by the common pattern of drivers beginning to board passengers while still in the queue, then pulling up, boarding more passengers, and sometimes pulling up and boarding again. In any event, the noise and fumes created by idling are noticeable and negatively affect the visitor experience. The high level of bus activity also tends to reduce the sense of solitude that is otherwise part of the Glacier experience.

5.2.4. Visual impacts

Bus activity in the teardrop area and associated visual clutter reduces the quality of the view toward the Glacier as originally designed. It also makes it difficult for the occasional visitor to determine appropriate routes for private vehicles.

6.0 Factors Contributing to Congestion

The primary reason for congestion at Mendenhall Glacier is insufficient capacity to meet visitation peak demand, which is principally determined by the number of cruise ships in port at any given time. Facility design, operator and passenger behavior, and weather conditions also contribute to vehicular and pedestrian congestion. The following sections outline factors contributing to congestion in each of these areas.

6.1 Relationship between cruise-ship dockings and MGVC traffic congestion

On the basis of observations of bus-passenger loading and unloading areas, MGVC staff have observed that the degree of traffic congestion on any given day is strongly correlated with the number of cruise ships docked in Juneau at that time. In this section, an attempt is made to extrapolate the numerical impacts of the cruise industry on visitation at Mendenhall Glacier.

Visitation patterns align closely with the tourism high season and are driven largely by the cruise-ship schedule. While the schedule changes slightly from season to season, it does not vary greatly within the season and generally repeats from week to week. Peaks tend to occur one to one and a half hours after a ship has docked, in the mid-morning and mid-afternoon. Tuesdays and Wednesdays were the busiest days for the 2006 season.

Figures 20 and 21 show this relationship throughout the season and over the course of the week. The total number of cruise-ship passengers, as estimated from an analysis of port activity, and the total number of visitors arriving at Mendenhall Glacier by tour-bus, shuttle, and taxi are compared.

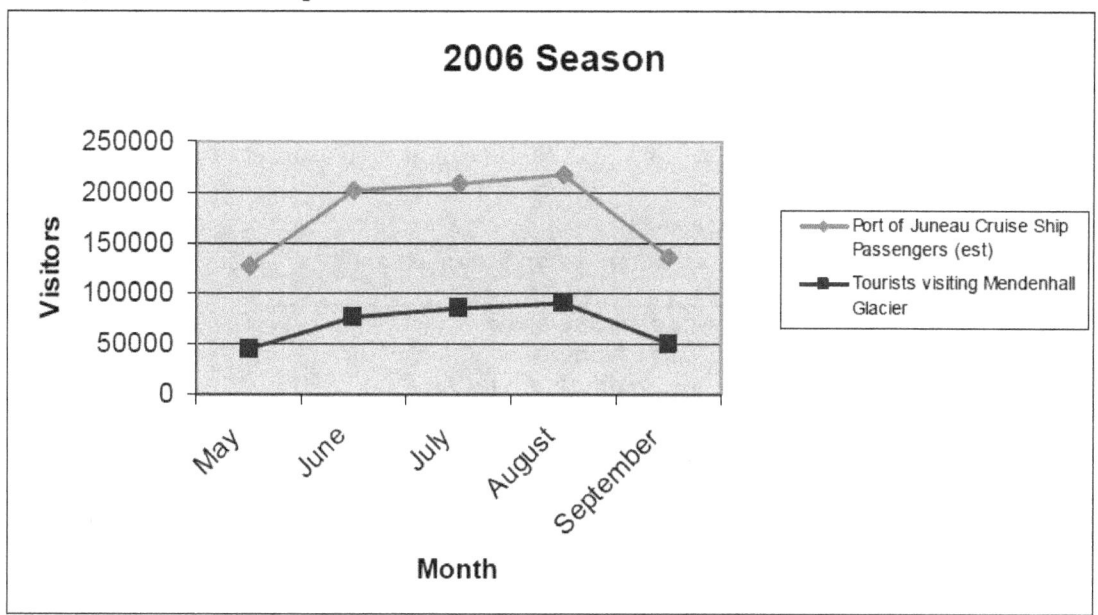

Figure 20: Relationship between visitation pattern and month.

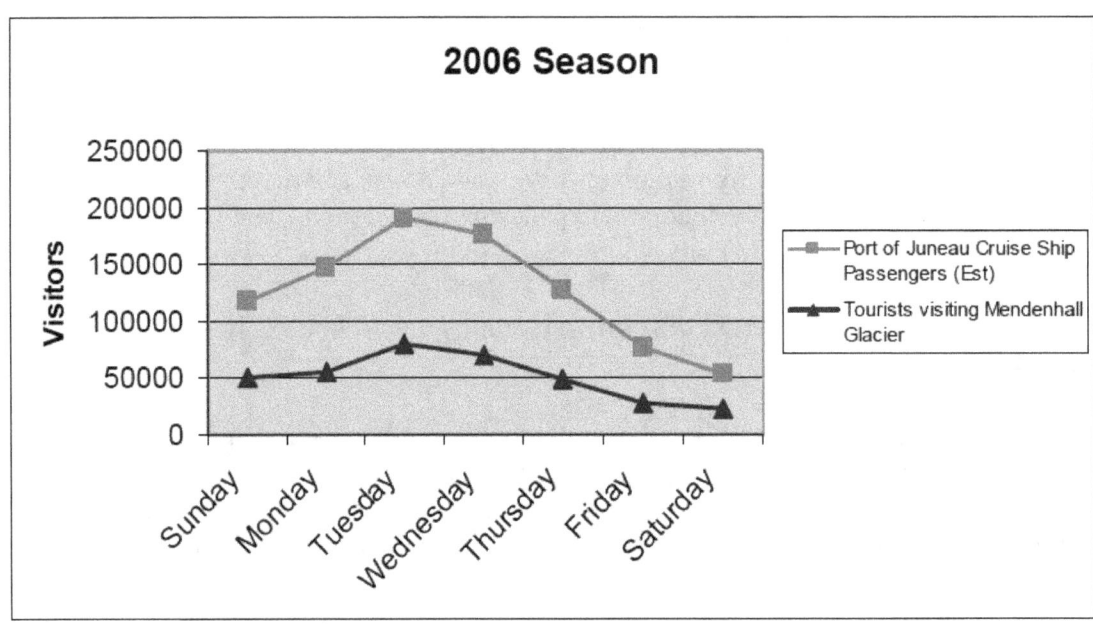

Figure 21: Relationship between visitation pattern and day of week.

Juneau's port can accommodate up to five ships of the size used by the major cruise lines. (The city government has indicated that, while there may be improvements or expansions of the docks, the number of cruise ships permitted in the harbor will continue to be capped at five.)

According to MGVC staff, the drop-off area is generally orderly and manageable on days when *no more than three* cruise ships are in port but is prone to become congested on days when four ships are docked. Days with five ships in port present the greatest issues with congestion and pedestrian-vehicle conflicts.

For this discussion, it may be more useful to think in terms of bus arrivals at MGVC rather than cruise-ship counts. Table 2 shows some calculations based on ship capacity and docking-schedule information for the 2006 season as well as a set of assumptions based on stakeholder interviews.

Table 2: Relationship between number of cruise-ship passengers and number visiting Mendenhall Glacier

No. of ships docked at Juneau	No. of cruise-ship passengers	No. of cruise-ship passengers visiting Mendenhall Glacier	No. of buses to MGVC
1	1,637	982	26
2	3,275	1,965	52
3	4,912	2,947	78
4	6,550	3,930	103
5	8,187	4,912	129

As an example, when four ships are in Juneau this means that approximately 6,550 cruise passengers are in Juneau on organized shore excursions, based on the average ship capacity of 1,819 passengers for the 2006 season and an estimated 90% take-up rate for excursions. About 60% of these passengers typically visit Mendenhall Glacier, which translates into 3,930 visitors, or about 103 busloads consisting of 38 people per full-sized motor coach. If the arrival of these buses were spread evenly over the course of a typical nine-hour visitation day (roughly 9 a.m. to 6 p.m.), this would mean that approximately 11 buses would arrive per hour.

Though based on rough calculations, these figures generally correspond to MGVC-collected data on visitor totals per day and bus arrivals per hour during the season. The figures are typical numbers based on *average* ship sizes and the assumption of an *even* flow of visitors to MGVC over the course of the day. In point of fact, some ships are larger than others, and bus tours to Mendenhall Glacier have some tendency to "bunch" during periods of day that coordinate with the overall cruise and excursion schedule. MGVC staff have recorded instances of 18 buses or more arriving in the course of an hour during these peak periods, and as might be expected, congestion and safety issues are most pronounced at these times.

These calculations suggest that, as a rule of thumb, the MGVC loading areas as currently configured can function smoothly when tour-bus arrivals are no more than nine per hour. Appendix II describes ways to increase this functional capacity, either through outright expansion of the loading areas or through traffic management.

6.2 Carrying capacity

It is also important to consider the carrying capacity of the area. The 1996 Mendenhall Glacier Recreation Area Management Plan Revision: Final Environmental Impact Statement (FEIS) allocates 65% of Visitor Center capacity for commercial use. This allows for a maximum of 462,190 visitors per summer season (defined as May 15–September 15), with an average of 3,370 visitors per day. This capacity is based on an average tour length of one hour; the FEIS notes that increasing the tour length may decrease capacity.

The "persons at one time" (PAOT) capacity, which is generally the more important figure in terms of visitor experience and congestion, has been estimated at 856 visitors. The point at which this PAOT capacity is exceeded depends on variables such as the average duration of a visit to MGVC and the degree to which group arrivals are concentrated during certain times of day. In addition, assuming a capacity of 856 PAOT and a one-hour stay over the period 9 a.m. to 6 p.m., 7,704 visitors could be accommodated. The actual daily capacity may lie somewhere between 3,730 and 7,704.

As Table 2 indicates, this figure will be exceeded by the number of cruise-based visitors alone whenever four or more ships are in port; the visitor total is even higher when independent tourists and local visitors are included.

Today, visitation remains under the seasonal limit established by the 1996 FEIS. In 2006, 358,172 visitors were brought by commercial operators. Nevertheless, due to the strong peaks in visitor arrivals related to the cruise-ship schedule, the Visitor Center complex experiences crowding and congestion. Visitor Center occupancy information is not available, but daily arrivals have exceeded the average daily capacity of 3,370 for the last several seasons.

Table 3: Days over nominal capacity, 2003–2006[6]

Days	2003	2004	2005	2006
Total no. of days per season	139	137	138	142
No. of days over capacity* (percent)	13 (9%)	22 (16%)	34 (25%)	26 (18%)

*More than 3,730 visitors.

6.3 Facility design and operational issues

The existing layout allows for a maximum of nine or ten buses engaged in pick-up or drop-off activity at three sites: three "Big 3" buses picking up, two shuttles or independent tours, and four or five "Big 3" buses dropping off. After these thresholds are met, the addition of further buses will create congestion. As noted above, the Glacier often receives more buses at each of these sites than can be comfortably accommodated in the bus areas and within the Visitor Center facilities.

Teardrop-area dimensions. The teardrop dimensions and the overall width of the circular drive constrain the movement of buses. Activity at the shuttle site constrains access to both the first parking lot and the exit from the "Big 3" pick-up area.

If more than two standard-sized independent buses were parked at the curb on the far side of the teardrop, the "Big 3" buses generally had trouble maneuvering around them, given the turning radius provided. In some cases, a multipoint turn provided enough space for the "Big 3" bus to pull around, but in several instances the bus had to wait until the independent buses pulled forward. Both solutions add delay, and the former causes a bus to reverse in an area crowded with pedestrians, an undesirable and unsafe situation.

First parking lot access. All of this activity may block private vehicle access to the first parking lot. While additional capacity exists in the second lot, drivers show a preference for the first lot and often drive past it to check for vacancies before ultimately parking in the second lot.

Passenger-count collection. Forest Service staff members collect passenger count information, to be used for special-permit per-person billings, with a handheld computer. This system has some benefits, as staff members build relationships with bus operators and it creates a wealth of data. However, it also adds a minimal amount of time to the total dwell time.

---

[6] Adapted from *Visitor Center Complex Capacity* document provided by USFS Juneau Region.

Visitor Center fee payment. Both prepaid and nonprepaid Visitor Center visitors use the same entrance. At peak times, this creates confusion and congestion as staff attempt to check wristbands that denote prepayment and direct visitors to the payment area as appropriate.

Visitor Center layout. The main activity areas of the Visitor Center—bookstore, information desk, and auditorium—are clustered at the entrance. The auditorium capacity is limited to 104, so visitors must queue at peak times to view the 11-minute film. Queues to enter the auditorium, to speak to a staff member at the information desk, and to make purchases at the bookstore interfere with circulation during times of high visitation.

6.4 Operator behavior

Operators contribute to the level of congestion and to a hazardous pedestrian environment. The Forest Service has the ability to regulate operator behavior through the special-permit process. Some practices that contribute to congestion are discussed in this section.

Crowding in the shuttle area. From the queue, especially as it lengthens, it is fairly difficult for shuttle operators to assess activity and space availability. Shuttle-bus and independent-tour operators were frequently observed proceeding to the area when it was already full, causing the types of backups described above. This indicates both that the area is insufficiently large to meet the demand for space and that these operators may require more training and regulation.

Arriving early. Observers did not have information on bus pick-up and could not measure their "on-time" performance. However, buses were observed to occasionally arrive at the pick-up or shuttle areas when their parties were not yet assembled, suggesting that the bus was early.

Backing up. As noted above, during periods of congestion at the shuttle area "Big 3" buses frequently experienced difficulty in maneuvering around the shuttles to exit the teardrop area. Some drivers chose to execute a multipoint turn, requiring them to reverse in an area crowded with pedestrians. Given the high number of pedestrians, this is not desirable even at the slow speeds used.

Leaving the vehicle. At both the "Big 3" drop-off area and the shuttle area, at least one driver was observed to exit the vehicle and leave the immediate area. The consequences were severe, with multiple buses stacking up behind the abandoned vehicle. While this is likely not a common occurrence, it is entirely avoidable.

Handing out wristbands before or during off-loading. "Big 3" drivers are instructed to pass out wristbands to their passengers as proof of payment for the Visitor Center entry fee before arriving at the Glacier. However, some drivers were observed passing out wristbands once the vehicle was stopped in the drop-off area but before or during the off-loading process. These practices lengthen dwell times.

Boarding a bus in the queue. This issue is really one of facility design, driver behavior, and passenger behavior. The distinction between the three striped spaces in the allotted "Big 3" boarding area and the queue is not easily seen by passengers. Once they spot their bus in the queue, they frequently proceed to it and attempt to board. Drivers ultimately bear the responsibility, as they make the decision to open the doors and begin boarding. This is problematic, as it encourages passengers to walk in front of and around buses. The queued area is also accessed from a dirt shoulder and is not fully accessible.

Stopping short. At all three sites, drivers frequently failed to make efficient use of the space, stopping before they had fully pulled up. Often, the area would be fairly quiet when the driver did so, but newly arriving buses would rapidly back up behind the bus in question.

Not pulling fully into the space. Drivers sometimes failed to pull their vehicle fully up to the curb, leaving the rear of the vehicle in the travel lane. This either blocked or complicated the movement of vehicles in the travel lane.

Both stopping short and not pulling all the way into the space were problematic in the second parking lot. As this lot was not designed for bus operations, the curb configuration is somewhat awkward. Drivers displayed a preference to pull the front of the bus up to particular spots. Stopping in these spaces allowed the driver to minimize the distance from the vehicle to the curb, making alighting easier, especially for mobility-challenged patrons. However, this preference sometimes caused drivers to make less efficient use of the space by not pulling up fully or by leaving the rear of the bus in the travel lane.

6.5 Passenger behavior

Of the contributing factors, passenger behavior is the one that the Forest Service has the least ability to control. An understanding of passenger characteristics is useful for evaluation of possible remedies.

Returning to the bus after alighting. In several cases, drop-off dwell times were lengthened by passengers returning to their buses after alighting to retrieve or store personal effects or to ask questions of the driver.

Walking between buses. Pedestrian "desire lines," or desired routes, as seen in Figure 22, go directly through the shuttle and "Big 3" pick-up areas. While many visitors used the sidewalks provided, many others did not. In addition, "Big 3" passengers walked in between and around buses while attempting to locate their bus. This behavior increases the possibility of a vehicle-pedestrian conflict.

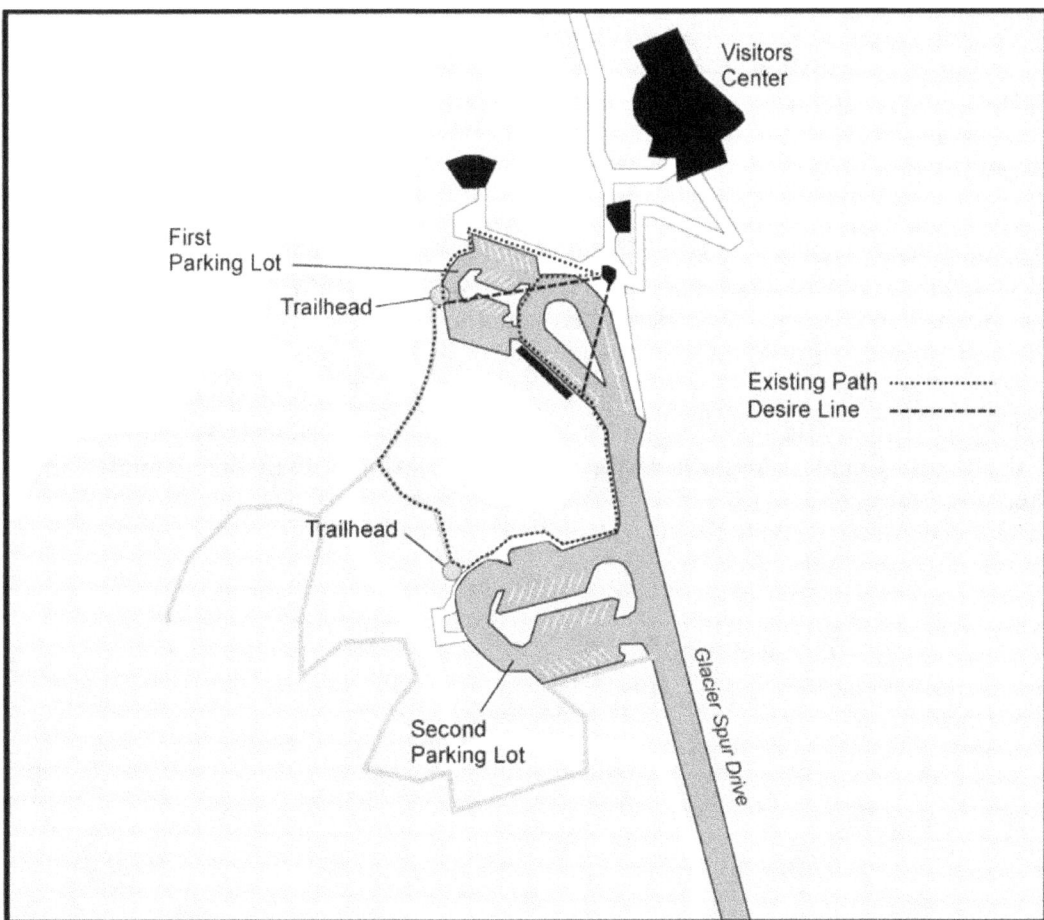

Figure 22: Pedestrian routes.

Being late for the bus. "Stragglers" are passengers who arrive at the bus pick-up area after the initial group has boarded. According to interviewees, the number of "stragglers" and passengers left behind seems to have increased in each of the past years. This can lead to longer dwell times on pick-ups because people can be late in arriving at the pick-up point (or be in the wrong place), and it takes time to round up "stragglers" and confirm that everyone is aboard. In a few cases, boarded passengers got off the bus to look for their companions, and in some instances drivers left without passengers if they could not be located and the bus needed to proceed to its next destination.

The last two issues are closely related to a lack of passenger information, as described in the previous section.

Passengers boarding the wrong bus. This was particularly common in the shuttle area. Many companies operate both independent tours and shuttle buses. Members of tour groups inadvertently boarded a shuttle bus operated by the same company, and shuttle passengers inadvertently boarded the tour buses. Passengers also boarded buses belonging to the "wrong" companies. In all cases, this caused delay while passengers spoke with the driver and off-loaded before other passengers could board.

Arriving early at the pick-up area and crowding it. When passengers arrived in advance of their pick-up time, the area rapidly became crowded, making it more difficult for other passengers to locate and reach their buses for boarding.

6.6 Weather conditions

Weather conditions affect MGVC visitation in three ways. First, popular excursions, including helicopter tours, flight-seeing, and whale watching, may be cancelled due to adverse weather conditions. Visitors booked onto these excursions are often rerouted to Mendenhall Glacier. Second, in rainy weather, visitors make more use of the covered viewing areas and the Visitor Center, leading to crowding. Finally, local residents are much more likely to visit MGVC when the weather is good. On these days, crowding inside the Visitor Center is less of a concern, although parking of personal vehicles may spill over onto the access road.

7.0 Ancillary Issues

Stakeholder interviews elicited several other issues related to visitation and facility design. While these are not directly related to congestion, they are noted here because they will shape the development of alternatives.

7.1 Accessibility

Accessibility for all is an important issue for any public space. Given the demographics of the cruise industry, which attracts an elderly population, accessibility for those with mobility impairments is particularly important at Mendenhall Glacier. The Visitor Center is fully accessible, with an elevator and a ramp from the ground level; however, visitors may benefit from improved signage and other visual cues to locate the elevator.

Steep Creek Trail, which was not designed for primary access, has become the de facto path for tour-bus passengers to use after being dropped off in the second parking lot. While the entrance to the trail is accessible, it culminates in a narrow stairway at the first parking lot. Placement of a ramp and perhaps a wider stairway would improve usability for all.

The distance from the drop-off and pick-up areas to the main facilities is also of concern. There is a fully accessible sidewalk running from the second parking lot to the main area. Where it passes through the shuttle pick-up and drop-off area, however, it is prone to congestion. Bus drivers varied in their response to this issue, with some dropping off all passengers, including those in wheelchairs or with limited mobility, in the second parking lot and others dropping passengers off in the pick-up area on request.

7.2 Wayfinding

Since the current pick-up and drop-off configuration is something of a pilot, the Forest Service was understandably reluctant to invest in permanent signage. This has led to visitor confusion, especially as locations cannot be easily understood visually from some of the current points of entry. The temporary signage is small in size and may not be sufficient to orient passengers.

After being dropped off in the second parking lot, visitors emerge from Steep Creek Trail at the rear of the first parking lot, which is somewhat disorienting. While the Glacier itself is easily seen, the Visitor Center was designed and constructed above ground-level and set back into the cliff so as to be unobtrusive and not compete visually with the Glacier. While the design succeeds from this standpoint, visitors need additional information to find the Visitor Center.

More information about the length, accessibility, and difficulty of the trails would likely be appreciated by visitors as well.

7.3 Environmental impacts

7.3.1. Idling and emissions

As noted above, although idling is prohibited by the terms of the special permit, some drivers continue to run their engines while queuing or boarding passengers. Consequently, fumes are present in the immediate pick-up and drop-off areas. Air-quality analysis may be useful in determining the extent of any impact to the larger area, including the Glacier.

7.3.2. Motor oil

Motor oil was observed in all of the pick-up and drop-off areas. Like idling, leaking oil is formally prohibited by the special permit, but enforcement is difficult as linking oil to a particular vehicle or company is nearly impossible.

7.3.3. Habitats

Conversations with Forest Service staff revealed some concern that increased human and vehicular activity in the second parking lot may negatively affect animal populations, particularly bears feeding upon salmon in Steep Creek. Other staff contended that, as this is a Visitor Center designed for people, wildlife will adapt to the increased activity or move away from the immediate area. While this impact is outside the expertise of the Volpe Center, further analysis by a qualified party may be required.

8.0 Stakeholder Viewpoints

8.1 Summary of interviews

Interviews were conducted with Forest Service staff members at Mendenhall Glacier, the Juneau District, Tongass National Forest, and the Alaska Region Office as well as with the Alaska Department of Transportation, the City and Borough of Juneau, tour operators and bus drivers, and operators of other tourist venues in Juneau.[7]

Summary
Interviewees stressed the importance of Mendenhall Glacier to Juneau residents and to the tourism industry alike. While it is the premier destination for Juneau visitors, the local community also feels a great deal of "ownership" for Mendenhall Glacier, and any changes that would tend to reduce their access to and enjoyment of the area would not be well received.

In general, stakeholders felt that vehicular congestion was somewhat less problematic than in previous years due to the expanded capacity offered by the pilot operations for the 2006 season. Views were split on the elimination of active traffic management by the USFS. Some drivers and operators did not like being managed by the Forest Service; others felt that management was helpful and would rather see it reinstated. The lack of active traffic management was noted to contribute to buses arriving early, staying in the loading areas longer, and not respecting the traffic rules.

The general view of interviewees was that visitors found wayfinding somewhat more difficult than in previous years. Some commented that the location of curbside pick-ups and drop-offs along the teardrop seems to engender pedestrian-vehicle conflicts.

Tour operators
- Primary concerns were the ease of passenger loading and unloading and the consistency of pedestrian and shuttle traffic.
- Operators noted that the amount of traffic at the Visitor Center is too big to self-regulate, and they believed that the Forest Service should provide a staff member to do so. They strongly rejected the concept of staffing a bus management position at the Visitor Center, as they felt that such a position should be subsidized by the special-permit fees they already pay. In addition, they felt that other companies might not respect the direction of a staff member from a company not their own.
- One interviewee noted that the Visitor Center is too crowded.

---

[7] A full list of interviewees can be found in Appendix I.

City and Borough of Juneau

- Mendenhall Glacier is one of the premier destinations in Juneau and Southeast Alaska.
- Juneau has nearly reached capacity as far as the number of cruise passengers it can accommodate, and the industry is starting to look to other destinations.
- The transit agency's mission is to serve the local population; there is little support locally for trying to accommodate tourists on transit buses. Additionally, the agency does not want to compete with the private sector. Occasionally, tourists crowd buses; this is negatively perceived by the local population.
- Tourism is a huge industry, and opinion is split locally. It is critical to the economy, but negative impacts, primarily helicopter noise, are unwelcome.
- The Glacier has a big role in local recreation. It is a popular spot for sledding, ice-skating, cross-country skiing, and hiking. The fireside chats are also very popular.

Visitors

Visitors were not directly interviewed, but comment cards were reviewed to extract comments relevant to the transportation system. Visitor comment cards tend to reflect the extremes of visitor opinion, as visitors must be motivated to fill them out, and they may not accurately capture the opinions of the majority. The most frequent transportation-related comment was the need to improve accessibility for the mobility-impaired, followed by concerns about crowding and wayfinding and a desire for city buses to run out to the Glacier.

Relevant excerpts from visitor comment cards:

- "You need to make the covered viewing area handicap-accessible. People are becoming upset. Also, you should give directions at the drop-off point."
- "Five buses completely blocked the parking and turnaround area. I guess if you live here you cannot view the Glacier. You need a better plan."
- "I feel that you could provide for easier access to handicapped people, such as a ride to this building so they could view the Glacier."
- "Tell tour-bus drivers to inform tourists to visit the Center *first*."
- "Please do everything possible to make this park *quieter!* We could not believe the noise level from tour buses and helicopters overhead. Mandate electric trolleys or buses!"

Forest Service

Interviews were conducted with many Forest Service personnel representing several offices within the Alaska Region. Consequently, a wide range of opinions, many conflicting, was heard. In general, conflicting opinions can be summarized as a question of access: should all visitors who wish to visit be able to do so, or should visitation limits be put into place to improve the experience for those who do come?

Some were concerned with the impacts of increased human activity on Steep Creek Trail wildlife; others were not. There was general consensus that bus activity in the teardrop

---

area negatively impacts the visitor experience by blocking views of the Glacier and creating noise and emissions, although views were split on the seriousness of these impacts. Several Forest Service interviewees stressed the importance of preserving or enhancing glacial views and creating a sense of arrival for visitors. Some Forest Service staff objected to increasing the paved area; others were open to the possibility. All interviewees agreed that filling in the kettle ponds or other wetlands would not be desirable.

Recommendations from other agencies
Representatives of the Federal Transit Administration, National Park Service, Federal Lands Highway, and USFS Washington office provided input into alleviating the congestion issues at Mendenhall Glacier in a web conference held November 13, 2006. Their input can be found in Appendix I.

9.0 Summary of Approaches Considered

Transportation patterns to and from the Glacier are resulting in four main issues: vehicular congestion, pedestrian congestion (inside and outside), safety, and erosion of the visitor experience quality. A wide range of approaches to these issues was developed and analyzed for applicability to the site. The approaches fall into eight main categories, as shown below. In each category, multiple strategies for achieving the goal were created and analyzed. One approach to the problem might be changing the entire transportation system by creating new access modes from Juneau to the Recreation Area (see number 6 below). A strategy that was considered was creating a new fixed-guideway transit system. However, this strategy is expensive, requires many years to implement, and fundamentally solves the wrong problem, as congestion is not experienced en route but rather at the terminus. Consequently, this strategy was not brought forward as an alternative.

The results of the strategy analysis were used to create the short- and long-term alternatives that appear in Section 10. A brief summary of findings appears in this section. (See Appendix II for more detail on the individual strategies considered.)

9.1 Approaches

1. Increase space for bus operations.
This approach would resolve congestion by expanding space for bus operations. Strategies using either existing facilities or developing new areas were considered.
- The existing paved areas can be redesigned to improve pedestrian and vehicular flows, but there is no workable design that creates significant additional bus-loading capacity without expanding the paved footprint.
- There are relatively few candidate sites for bus facilities within a comfortable walking distance of the Visitor Center.
- Locating bus activity at sites not within walking distance of the Visitor Center will require an additional internal circulation system (see number 8 below).
- The Visitor Center is at or over capacity during peak times in the season. Increasing transportation capacity without increasing visitor capacity will have a negative impact on the visitor experience.

2. Maximize efficiency of bus activity areas.
This approach seeks to make the existing bus activity areas more efficient, improving capacity and reducing congestion.
- Management strategies can be used to reduce dwell times and improve turnover of bus loading and unloading areas.
- The Visitor Center is at or over capacity during peak times in the season. Increasing transportation capacity without increasing visitor capacity will have a negative impact on the visitor experience.

3. Control access to bus activity areas.

This approach reduces congestion (and improves safety) by regulating vehicular access to the bus activity areas.

- Existing facilities can be managed to regulate the flow of bus traffic to loading and unloading areas, reducing vehicular and pedestrian congestion.

4. Reduce vehicular speeds along Glacier Spur Road.

Reducing vehicular speeds improves safety for drivers, other visitors, and wildlife.

- Traffic-calming techniques can improve safety and may add to the visitor's sense of arrival.

5. Reduce pedestrian-vehicle conflict points.

Reducing conflict points improves safety for all and clarifies site design for pedestrians, improving the quality of their experience.

- Operational and design strategies should minimize or eliminate the use of reversing by buses and provide a clear separation of uses. Differences in vehicle size and different types of movements make mixed traffic more likely to produce accidents.
- Bus activity areas should be clearly demarcated.
- Pedestrian routes should be designed to be clear and efficient. Pedestrians are likely to ignore designated routes if they are circuitous.

6. Introduce new access modes from Juneau to the Recreation Area.

New access modes could allow the Forest Service more control over vehicle flows and open up potential partnerships with the community.

- The existing transportation system transports a high number of visitors at no cost to the Forest Service and is extremely "efficient" in the sense that most visitors arrive via fully loaded, full-size coaches. Any shuttle system relying solely on smaller vehicles would require so many extra vehicles as to be counterproductive.
- High-capacity transport systems would overload existing facilities by "dumping" large numbers of visitors at one time.
- Congestion exists primarily at the bus loading and unloading areas rather than en route.

7. Introduce new access points to the Recreation Area.

- The focal point for tourists is the Visitor Center and the trails and observation areas immediately adjacent to it. Unless new facilities were to be developed, any circulation system must terminate within walking distance of the Visitor Center. Given the Visitor Center's position in between water and cliffs, the choices for a possible terminus location are fairly limited.

8. Create new circulation systems within the Recreation Area.

- Locating loading and unloading areas beyond a comfortable walking distance of the Visitor Center or developing new destinations for visitors will require the creation of new circulation systems within the Recreation Area.

- Internal circulation can be used to regulate the flow of visitors and/or to provide interpretation.

9.2 Evaluation Criteria

Evaluation criteria, below, were developed with the Forest Service. As the goal of this study was to identify feasible alternatives, they are presented at the conceptual level. Further planning and design work is necessary for implementation. Consequently, criteria are largely qualitative in nature and are used to evaluate impacts relative to other options.

- Impacts on congestion
- Impacts on safety
- Costs of implementation
- Time required for implementation
- Stakeholders/partnerships
- Impacts on visitor experience
    - Interpretation (or other USFS programs)
    - Views
    - Sense of place
    - Sense of arrival
    - Visitor comfort
    - Impacts on accessibility
- Environmental impacts
    - Vehicle emissions
    - Amount of paved/impermeable surface
    - Impact on flora/fauna

10.0 Alternatives

On the basis of stakeholder input, observation, and analysis of data from the 2005 and 2006 seasons, it is clear that the site, as designed and operated during the 2006 season, cannot accommodate the current volumes of tour-bus arrivals. The site is also highly constrained: grade changes, wetlands, and viewsheds limit options for adding capacity through expanded bus facilities in the immediate Visitor Center area. In addition, as noted above, the Visitor Center is already over capacity for portions of the summer season. Alternatives that introduce additional tour-bus capacity without facility improvements are likely to have a significant negative impact on the visitor experience.

Changes that can be implemented to improve the MGVC transportation system fall into three main categories: (1) signage and wayfinding, (2) management and staffing, and (3) construction. Within each of those areas, minor, moderate, or major changes can be implemented, each resulting in varying degrees of improvement. To maximize benefits, some improvements should be implemented in each area. However, the appropriateness of all but the most minor construction improvements cannot be determined until the completion of the Mendenhall Recreation Area Management Plan because lasting physical changes to the site need to be made compatible with the long-term vision articulated in that plan.

Consequently, this study focuses on alternatives that can be implemented in the short term (zero to five years), with a separate discussion in Section 10.2 of options and considerations for longer-term solutions. The long-term planning process should examine the Recreation Area's resources and visitor profiles holistically to determine the appropriate direction.

10.1 Alternatives for short-term implementation

Congestion currently varies from day to day and hour to hour. In the short term, the most promising strategies are those that control the number of buses loading or unloading at one time. Alternative approaches at a variety of resource intensities were developed with the considerations below in mind.

- Visitor orientation is key; most visitors are coming to Mendenhall Glacier for the first time and have only one or two hours on site. Visitor information and other improvements to wayfinding are thus critical to all alternatives.
- For a subset of visitors, local residents, joggers, hikers, and others, the area is a regular and important feature in their lives. These local residents prefer convenient parking.
- For all visitors, sense of place, sense of arrival, and viewsheds should be preserved or strengthened.
- Safety is integral to all alternatives.
- All of the short-term alternatives are based on the idea of *not* imposing a "hard cap" on visitation other than what is specified in the 1996 FEIS. This is based on USFS managers' statements that MGVC is an urban site and that they prefer to be

able to accommodate any visitors who come to see the Glacier. (For a discussion of approaches to limiting capacity over the longer term, see Section 10.2.1.)

Summary of alternatives

For simplicity, the alternatives are presented as distinct options. In reality, of course, a good deal of flexibility exists, and elements of the various options are compatible with each other. Appendix II presents the full range of approaches and strategies considered by the team. As long-term planning proceeds, elements from the full range may become more attractive.

- **Option A: No action/status quo.** 2006 operations are used as the baseline for evaluation.
- **Option B: 2006+.** The most conservative of the action alternatives, this option comprises relatively minor wayfinding and construction improvements, with active traffic management by traffic control aides enforcing new operational guidelines.
- **Option C: Interceptor lot.** The original traffic flow would be restored in most respects, an additional pick-up space would be created on the western side of the teardrop, and the bus lot would be used as a staging area to control traffic flow to and from the teardrop.
- **Option D: Reservation system.** As in Option C, the original traffic flow would be restored, but an advance reservation system would be used to moderate peak vehicular and pedestrian congestion.
- **Option E: Lot 2.** In this option, all bus activity would be relocated to the second parking lot and an electric tram would be added to improve accessibility of the Visitor Center for those with mobility constraints.

10.1.1. Option A: No Action/Status Quo

This alternative is to be used as a baseline for comparing the other alternatives. Under this alternative, traffic flows in and around MGVC would be regulated in the same manner as during the 2006 season, with largely the same results. However, visitation to Juneau is expected to rise by about 4% in 2007, which would put additional strain on traffic operations.

10.1.2. Option B: 2006+

This alternative would employ a number of small adjustments and traffic management techniques to improve the safety of visitors and reduce congestion. It is the most conservative of the "action" alternatives in that it assumes that the current (2006) roadway layout and traffic flow pattern would be preserved in most respects. It also would require no major construction and thus could be implemented more quickly than the other alternatives.

One recommended change to 2006 operations is that all tour buses would be co-located so that independent-tour operators would follow the drop-off and pick-up patterns used by the "Big 3" in 2006. By reducing the number of vehicles using the two spaces near the kettle pond, there is less likelihood that vehicles would queue at the exit to Lot 1 and block vehicles trying to leave the teardrop. This change would impact passenger counts and fee collection as performed today, so a pilot program to allow self-reporting by independent-tour operators is suggested.

Minor changes are proposed in each of the three categories: signage and wayfinding, management and staffing, and construction.

Signage and wayfinding
Additional wayfinding and interpretive signage would be installed at the base of Steep Creek Trail near the drop-off point for buses. This would create slightly more of a sense of arrival and would help visitors to find their way to the Glacier and the Visitor Center more easily. Additional directional signage would be placed along the entrance road and the teardrop to help motorists understand the traffic flow patterns and the location of parking and drop-off points for different vehicles. This would be of particular benefit to first-time visitors attempting to navigate the area in their own cars.

- Loading and unloading areas and passenger waiting areas should be clearly identified, with written information posted on "What to do if you miss your bus."

Management and staffing
Active traffic management, with one or more staff members focused on directing visitor and vehicular traffic, can significantly improve traffic flows and safety. Traffic control staffers are a common sight at any facility that receives a large number of buses, including some national parks such as Denali and Yosemite. Indeed, MGVC itself has used employees to provide traffic control in prior years. The very presence of such staff

can help to promote safety and relieve congestion in a number of ways, such as orienting bus drivers, helping drivers to reverse safely or negotiate tight spaces, and serving as a point of contact and advice for visitors. In this alternative, traffic control staff would be valuable not only for those roles but also for putting some "teeth" into the operational guidelines described below and managing traffic.

On the basis of interviews with stakeholders, it appears that the most workable option would be for these traffic control staff to be employed by USFS rather than by the tour operators. Since reassigning interpretive staff to traffic control duties would represent an obvious mismatch in resources and capabilities, a better option would be to recruit seasonal staff who would be specifically assigned to traffic control as their primary job responsibility. On the basis of the experience of other federal lands, employing traffic control staff would cost the Forest Service approximately $18,000 per employee per season (May-September) for salary and benefits. At current visitation levels, the cost of employing four or five traffic control aides could be covered by a small increase in the permit or entrance fees (less than $0.50 per visitor).

Traffic control staff could be used for the primary purpose of regulating tour buses, assisting visitors, or both. If both functions are desired, more staff are needed. If staff are desired only to regulate tour buses, they should be positioned in the bus loading areas, away from visitor pedestrian areas. This is because "official-looking" individuals are magnets for visitor questions and as visitors flock to them for guidance, they will invariably be unable to perform their tour-bus-management duties. If both tour-bus management and visitor guidance are desired, it is recommended that more staff be employed to cover these functions.

Operational guidelines can be integrated with minor physical changes to enhance the operation of the space. To implement these changes, procedures should be added as stipulations under the commercial operator special-permit process. Bringing operators together to discuss the new policies in advance of the 2007 season is recommended as well.

- Facilitate vehicle identification.
  - o All for-hire vehicles serving MGVC must prominently display the company name, unique name or number of the vehicle, and type of service (shuttle or tour) on their exterior to make it easier for visitors to identify their vehicle.
  - o Similarly, tour-bus drivers should wait outside of their vehicle, actively greeting passengers while they board whenever possible. Since many visitors remember their driver but not their vehicle, this will help visitors to identify the correct bus prior to boarding.

Both of these policies will reduce the confusion and delays that occur when visitors are unable to locate their bus or attempt to board the wrong vehicle.

- Prevent vehicles from waiting for late arrivals.

- o Vehicles are limited to 10 minutes for pick-up.[8] Buses would have to vacate their space, leaving passengers behind if necessary.
- o As part of their tour packets, passengers should be provided with printed information on what to do if they are left behind at the Glacier. This might include a dispatcher's phone number and information on transportation options for returning to downtown Juneau. This might alleviate some of the anxiety that visitors experience about the possibility of missing their bus. Additionally, signage with access to communication (pay phone) should be provided, with clear instructions about what visitors should do if they miss their bus.

- ▪ Drivers should understand that they are to open the bus door only once and only in the designated location.
  - o Vehicles may pick up and drop off only in spaces specifically marked and designated for this purpose.
  - o Vehicles are prohibited from moving up into empty spaces after beginning to board passengers, as this process can significantly extend the amount of time it takes to board the vehicle and can add to visitor confusion. To speed boarding, the door of the bus should be opened only once, with all passengers boarding at that time rather than allowing small groups of passengers to board at various points along the roadway.
  - o No passengers shall be allowed to board outside of designated loading areas. When passengers board at various points along the roadway, it causes congestion, increases safety hazards, confuses others about where they should proceed to board their bus, and increases the time it takes to load vehicles, all of which perpetuate congestion.
  - o No bus may enter the teardrop without being called forward by the traffic control officer, nor may buses wait in the hashed "no stopping" area behind the last pick-up space.

Construction
- ▪ One or more flexible plastic bollards, to be located behind the second shuttle/independent pick-up space along the teardrop (Figure 23), would help to prevent a third vehicle from attempting to move into this space for pick-up or drop-off. This would reduce the congestion that occurs when a third vehicle stops in this location, thus preventing rearward vehicles from leaving the teardrop due to the narrowed turning radius. (The flexible bollard would not damage a vehicle that accidentally drove into it, and it could be removed after peak season and placed in storage.)

- ▪ Additional pavement striping would be used to provide better demarcation of the boarding areas along the teardrop and to create a hashed "no stopping or standing" area to the rear of the last pick-up space (Figure 23). This would discourage buses

---

[8] Meeting with tour operators to assess their comfort with this time limit is recommended. While the median pick-up time for the "Big 3" was eight minutes and much lower for other operators, "field-testing" this limit may be necessary.

from queuing in the area, reducing confusion and the conflicts and congestion that occur when passengers leave the teardrop area to attempt to board their bus farther down the road. Prior to the start of the season, the USFS would inform tour operators that their drivers may not use this area.

- Similarly, a pedestrian railing or gate across the sidewalk at the end of the boarding area would encourage passengers to wait in the designated boarding area rather than attempt to board their bus farther down the road.

- The Mendenhall Glacier "Welcome" sign would be removed from the teardrop in order to eliminate pedestrian safety issues that occur when visitors cross the road to have their picture taken by the sign. The sign could be relocated to an area where the space is more conducive to photo opportunities and there are no conflicts with motor vehicles, perhaps closer to the Visitor Center.

- The narrow stairway leading from Steep Creek Trail to the first parking lot would be widened and a wheelchair-accessible ramp would be added.

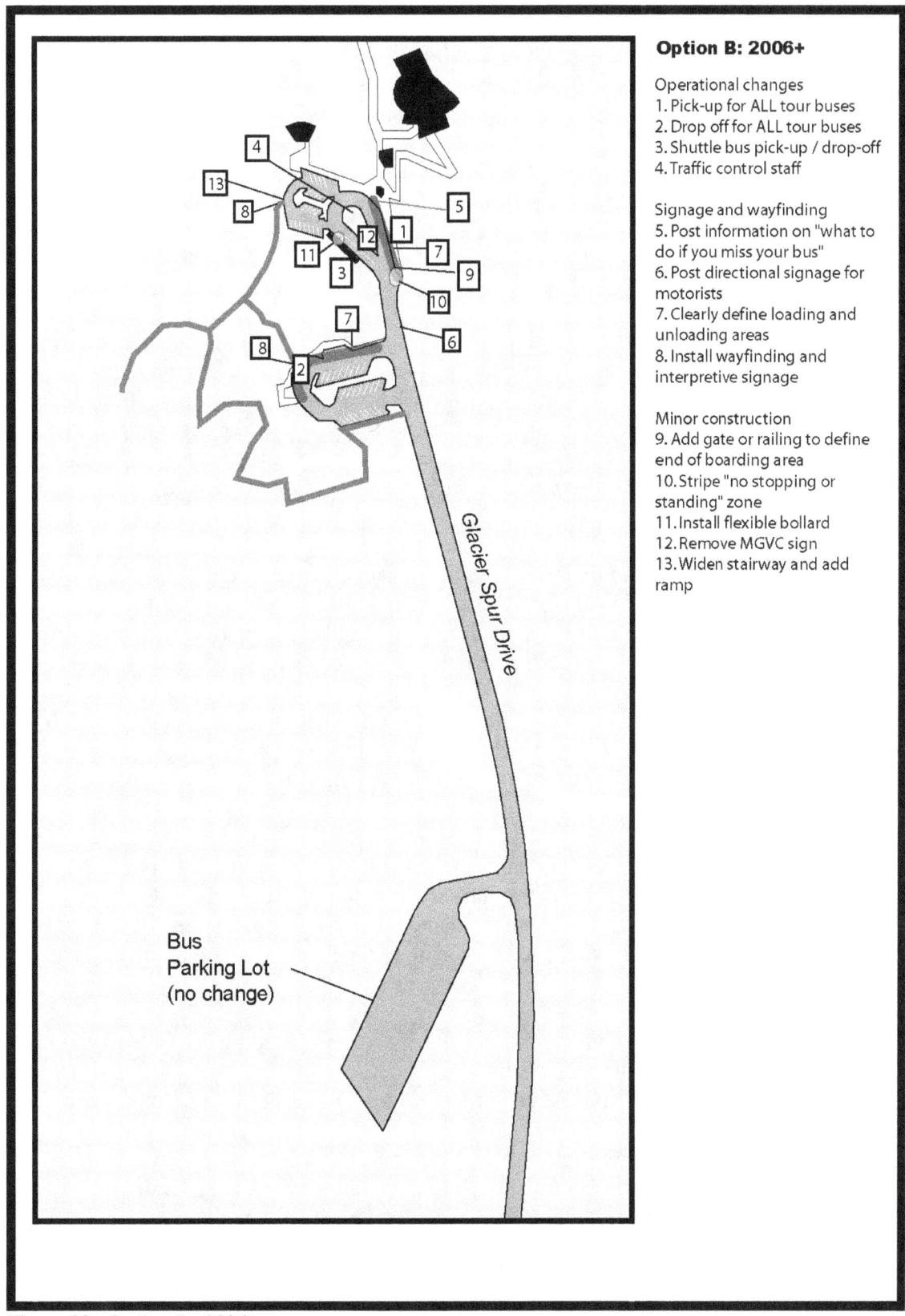

Option B: 2006+

Operational changes
1. Pick-up for ALL tour buses
2. Drop off for ALL tour buses
3. Shuttle bus pick-up / drop-off
4. Traffic control staff

Signage and wayfinding
5. Post information on "what to do if you miss your bus"
6. Post directional signage for motorists
7. Clearly define loading and unloading areas
8. Install wayfinding and interpretive signage

Minor construction
9. Add gate or railing to define end of boarding area
10. Stripe "no stopping or standing" zone
11. Install flexible bollard
12. Remove MGVC sign
13. Widen stairway and add ramp

Glacier Spur Drive

Bus Parking Lot (no change)

Figure 23: Option B: 2006+.

Evaluation

Many of these changes involve improving information and clarity for visitors and drivers. This approach is based on the fact that the majority of visitors to MGVC are "unique" visitors: they have never before been to Mendenhall Glacier. Consequently, clear, immediately understandable visual cues and systems are needed to orient them to the facility and keep them safe. Improving passenger information can reduce confusion, thereby enhancing the visitor experience, streamlining passenger boarding, and increasing safety by better separating traffic. Vehicle boarding times and the effective capacity of the loading area could also be improved by providing information that reduces the number of "stragglers."

The major advantage of this alternative is that the components could be implemented relatively quickly, in most cases before the next visitor season, at a low overall cost, though some elements would require lead time, planning, and expenditure. The addition of traffic control staff, though it comes at a cost, brings the potential for significant additional benefit in terms of traffic control, congestion mitigation, safety, and visitor experience. This alternative also does not require any increase in paved area or disruptive construction work.

This alternative will have a minor-to-moderate impact on congestion. It involves active traffic management by staff and clarification of conditions for visitors. Both are important to improving the existing situation but are unlikely to resolve it entirely. An additional drawback of this approach is that the continued or increased use of the second parking lot for bus drop-offs places pressure on a trail system that was not designed as a primary means of pedestrian access. The passage of large numbers of people through this area could have a detrimental impact on nearby salmon streams or other sensitive flora and fauna. It also changes the nature of the visitor experience along this section of the trail.

In general, the elements of this alternative are compatible with and do not preclude the use of more aggressive strategies in the future. This suggests the possibility of a conservative wait-and-see approach; these changes could be implemented within the next season or two and the results evaluated before more far-reaching changes are considered.

Pros:
- Expedites boarding times and improves operation of loading and unloading areas.
- Reduces potential for pedestrian-vehicle conflicts.
- Reduces pedestrian congestion at Steep Creek Trail stairway and improves accessibility.
- Relieves pressure from shuttle area and ensures accessibility of Lot 1.
- Reduces confusion in bus activity areas and along Steep Creek Trail.
- Conservative; does not rule out more comprehensive future changes.
- Will likely be acceptable to operators.
- Results in no net change in private vehicle parking.

Cons:
- Retains three separate bus activity areas, which may be confusing for visitors.
- Continues to mix tour and shuttle traffic.
- Still difficult for mobility-impaired visitors to move from Lot 2 to Visitor Center.
- Continued negative impacts along Steep Creek Trail.
- No impact on crowding within Visitor Center.
- Vehicle queuing still likely to occur, although wait times may be shortened.

Implementation:
- Costs of hiring, training, and maintaining additional seasonal staff members; implementing minor construction; and designing, creating, and installing directional signage.
- Minimal lead time required.

10.1.3 Option C: Interceptor Lot

This alternative takes a more aggressive approach to controlling bus traffic. An interceptor lot, controlled by USFS traffic aides, would be used to "meter" the flow of tour buses and shuttles to the teardrop, allowing only as many buses as could be accommodated at one time. The interceptor lot would be located in the gravel lot currently used for bus parking.

The teardrop also would be returned to something akin to its original layout, with bus drop-offs on the east side and pick-ups on the west side. A third bus pick-up space would be created through minor construction at the narrow end of the teardrop (pending environmental review) in order to increase the capacity of the system. There would be no change to traffic flows or parking locations for taxis and private vehicles.

The basic concept of the interceptor lot is that arriving buses do not proceed directly to the drop-off point but are held in the lot until a space becomes available, thus reducing congestion, confusion, and visual clutter at the drop-off point. In order to realize the maximum benefit, the interceptor strategy would be used to regulate the flow of buses not only on arrival but also between layover and pick-up.

Interceptor-lot rules would be in effect during peak periods. Traffic control staff (see Section 10.1.2) would monitor and direct the flow of buses between the interceptor lot and the pick-up and drop-off areas, using two-way radio communication (or push-to-talk cell phones). The traffic aides would order buses to "hold" in the layover lot until they could verify that a drop-off or pick-up space is or would shortly become available at the teardrop and then would instruct the bus driver to proceed.

To support this approach, the Forest Service would also convene a meeting with the operational staff of tour and shuttle companies to inform them of the new procedures as well as to discuss the possibilities for a common radio frequency to facilitate communication at the MGVC site. To date, operators have shown little enthusiasm for a common radio frequency, and it is assumed that most interaction between traffic control staff and drivers would be via direct conversation or hand and flag signals.

Directional signage would be posted along the entrance roadway, showing the location of the interceptor lot and the new traffic flow system. The Forest Service would also apply for funding to invest in intelligent transportation systems (ITS) that would support the work of traffic aides and automate part of the process. Parking-space sensors and traffic cameras could be used to provide information on conditions at the teardrop, and staff could remotely control a signal in the bus parking lot to indicate whether the next vehicle was cleared to proceed to the teardrop.

The use of interceptor lots often creates a delay for inbound visitors because at busy times their vehicle must wait at the lot until a space becomes available at the drop-off point. However, it is generally both safer and more pleasant for visitors if this delay occurred at the lot instead of at the more space-constrained and environmentally sensitive area near the Glacier. This is particularly true if the waiting time is used as an opportunity to provide a basic visitor orientation or some interpretive information. On the busiest days, when longer delays are likely, USFS interpretive staff would board the bus to provide visitors with a welcome and an introduction to the Glacier (assuming the availability of staff to perform this role). At other times, bus drivers would be provided with educational material to present to visitors while they wait for space to open in the loading-unloading area.

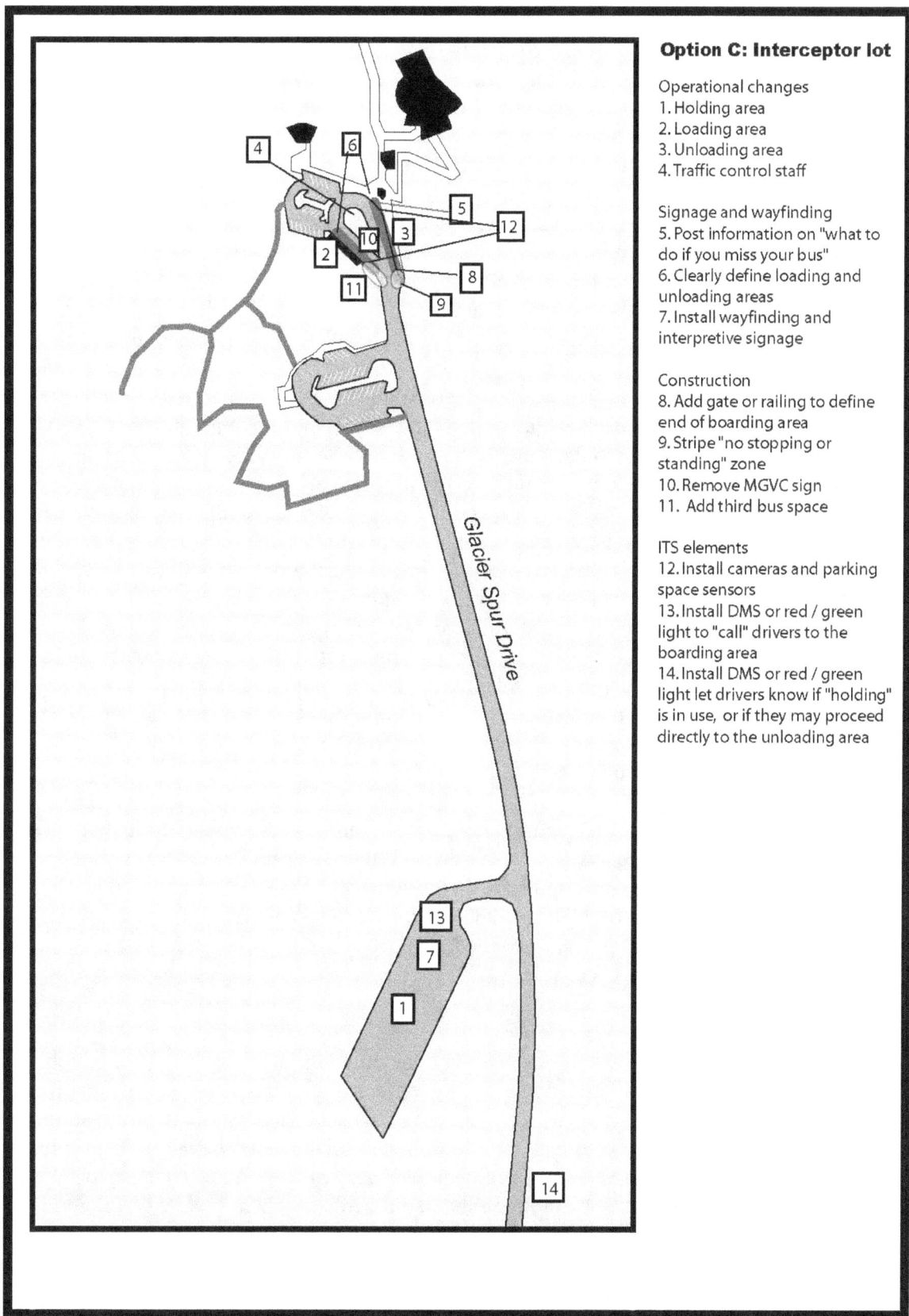

Option C: Interceptor lot

Operational changes
1. Holding area
2. Loading area
3. Unloading area
4. Traffic control staff

Signage and wayfinding
5. Post information on "what to do if you miss your bus"
6. Clearly define loading and unloading areas
7. Install wayfinding and interpretive signage

Construction
8. Add gate or railing to define end of boarding area
9. Stripe "no stopping or standing" zone
10. Remove MGVC sign
11. Add third bus space

ITS elements
12. Install cameras and parking space sensors
13. Install DMS or red / green light to "call" drivers to the boarding area
14. Install DMS or red / green light let drivers know if "holding" is in use, or if they may proceed directly to the unloading area

Glacier Spur Drive

Figure 24: Option C: Interceptor Lot.

Evaluation

The advantages of this approach are several. Congestion and tailpipe emissions would be reduced by use of the interceptor lot; delays that did occur would take place away from the Glacier and could be put to good use for visitor orientation and interpretation. In addition, the sense of arrival would be strengthened by reducing congestion in the teardrop area, and the visitor experience would be improved through more convenient access to the Glacier and Visitor Center on arrival. Compared with 2006 operations, visitor confusion would be reduced by having drop-off and pick-up take place within the same general area. This approach also offers the flexibility of being able to dispense with the interceptor lot altogether on off-peak and shoulder-season days when the volume of traffic is expected to be low. As the system would be in place only during peak periods, operators would have an incentive to adjust their schedules so as to arrive during off-hours.

One drawback of the approach is that visitors and tour operators might perceive the interceptor system to be an inconvenience and a source of needless delay. During periods when buses were being held before pick-up due to congestion, visitors might need to wait at the curb beyond their scheduled pick-up time, which would result in no improvement over existing conditions. There would also be delay between the release of buses from the interceptor lot and their arrival to occupy either the drop-off or pick-up space. Therefore, the percentage of time that the boarding or alighting spaces would be occupied would actually decrease under this alternative, leading to lower throughput. In addition, this system would have disproportionate impacts on shuttle-bus operators, who would be forced to add layover time into their schedules. There would also be the cost of hiring traffic control staff to run the interceptor lot system, though as mentioned above the cost of hiring several seasonal employees amounts to a very modest sum on a per-visitor basis and could be covered through a small increase in fees.

A more fundamental problem is that, although the interceptor lot would mitigate the effects of delays and move the problem away from the teardrop, it would do nothing to add to the capacity of the teardrop itself. In the short term, this would be an advantage as it would restricts the flow of visitors to the Visitor Center to manageable levels. However, a longer-term approach is needed to address the increase in visitors that is expected over the next two decades.

Note on Traffic Flow

The interceptor lot could be implemented with the existing (2006) traffic flow, which could still provide some improvement. However, this alternative is based on a modified version of the original teardrop layout. The virtue of that design is that it would allow for a greater sense of arrival as bus passengers alight near the Glacier viewshed. It would also be safer and more convenient, since visitors could reach the Visitor Center without crossing the busy roadway and could use the permanent rain shelter while waiting to be picked up. In addition, the original design alleviates the pressure on Steep Creek Trail as the second parking lot would not be used for drop-offs.

Despite these advantages, this layout was simply not designed to accommodate the number of visitors who now come to the Glacier during a typical summer day. The fact remains that the ability to load only two buses at once—or three buses, with this proposed minor construction—presents a limit on the capacity of the overall system, especially since the pick-up of a tour group typically takes longer than a drop-off. However, one of the primary benefits of this arrangement is that visitors would be immediately oriented on drop-off and would not be encouraged to walk across the teardrop area as they would be if they were dropped off on the western side. In addition, as noted above, operating the interceptor lot only during peak hours would give operators an incentive to modify their schedules so as to facilitate smooth arrivals.

Pros:
- Improves operation of loading and unloading areas.
- Reduces potential for pedestrian-vehicle conflicts.
- Creates more logical and convenient pedestrian flows.
- Relieves pressure from shuttle area and ensures accessibility of Lot 1.
- Breaks up flow of visitors into Visitor Center.
- Reduces visual clutter around teardrop.
- Improves wayfinding.
- Reduces bus idling and engine restarting.
- Achieves net gain in private vehicle parking (restores four or five spaces in Lot 2).
- Provides an incentive for operators to change schedules.

Cons:
- Continues to mix tour and shuttle traffic.
- Little reduction in overall vehicle waiting/queuing time (though location is changed).
- Possible decrease in throughput at loading/unloading areas.
- Accommodates only six active buses.
- Disproportionate impact on shuttle operators.
- Construction of additional bus pick-up space may negatively impact kettle ponds, soil, or other natural resources.

Implementation:
- Costs of hiring, training, and maintaining additional seasonal staff members; construction of additional bus pick-up space; posting of new signage; and acquisition of two-way communications.
- Meeting with tour- and shuttle-bus operators required.
- Minimal lead time except for ITS investments required.

10.1.4. Option D: Reservation System

This alternative would create a reservation system in which tour operators would be assigned specific drop-off and pick-up time slots as part of the special-permit application process. The number of slots available would be limited to the number of vehicles that could be accommodated without undue delay and congestion. This alternative would require hiring staff; constructing an additional pick-up space and an entry station; widening the roadway; developing, hosting, and implementing an online reservation system; and purchasing communications equipment.

An entry station would be constructed along Glacier Spur Road, and the roadway would be widened at this point to allow three lanes: one lane for entering commercial vehicles, one lane for entering private vehicles, and one lane for all exiting vehicles. The entry station could be staffed by either primary or traffic control staff. Traffic control staff would be hired to manage traffic and to update the system in real time.

The original teardrop layout, as modified in Section 10.1.3 to add a pick up space, would be used, with a total of three drop-off and three pick-up spaces available. Only four of the six spaces would be available for advance reservation; two would be left open to absorb impacts from late arrivals, overstay, or drivers arriving without a reservation. Arrivals would be scheduled at 10-minute intervals. Although dropping off requires significantly less time than picking up, equal time slots are recommended to balance arrivals and departures. Consequently, 24 time slots (12 drop-off and 12 pick-up) would be available for reservation each hour. Twelve busloads per hour at a maximum capacity of 55 passengers per bus would allow a maximum of 660 passengers per hour. Actual visitation would likely decrease due to the variety of vehicle sizes used by operators and the fact that passenger loads are typically somewhat less than maximum capacity. If a weighted median occupancy of 35 passengers per vehicle were used, it would allow for 423 passengers per hour.

Operators would request slots using an online form, and conflicting requests would be resolved either manually according to a set of predetermined rules or by use of scheduling software. Drivers would arrive at the entry station five minutes before their scheduled drop-off slot was to begin; they would check in and report on the number of passengers, then proceed to the teardrop area. A staffer at the entry station would update the system and alert traffic control staff that the vehicle was on its way. If a space were open, traffic control staff would direct the driver to it. Otherwise, the driver would queue until directed to move up. Queuing times would be minimal, as time slots would be relatively generous and staff would be present to enforce departure times for buses scheduled in the previous time slot. Use of the operational guidance described in Option B: 2006+ is also recommended.

After off-loading passengers, drivers would lay over in the bus lot, returning to the teardrop shortly before their scheduled pick-up time was to begin.

To further ensure that visitors would connect with their buses, a tour-bus status board would be located between the Visitor Center and the loading area and additional monitors would be placed in and by the front door of the Visitor Center. The informational displays would list the bus company, number, and status (standing by, boarding in "x" minutes, flashing "boarding" or "departed"), similar to displays found at airports and other transit terminals.

Under normal operating conditions, late arrivals would be directed to call in and receive a new arrival time. If none were available, the driver would be given the option to queue in the roadway until directed to move forward by traffic control staff. If widespread delay were caused by a ship arriving significantly late, all drivers would queue in the roadway and follow directions provided by traffic control staff. Some congestion is anticipated in this scenario. If operators were not going to arrive at all, they would notify staff at the Glacier as soon as possible. Drivers arriving without a reservation could queue with the understanding that they could not move up into the teardrop until one of the two "free" slots was available and they had been called forward.

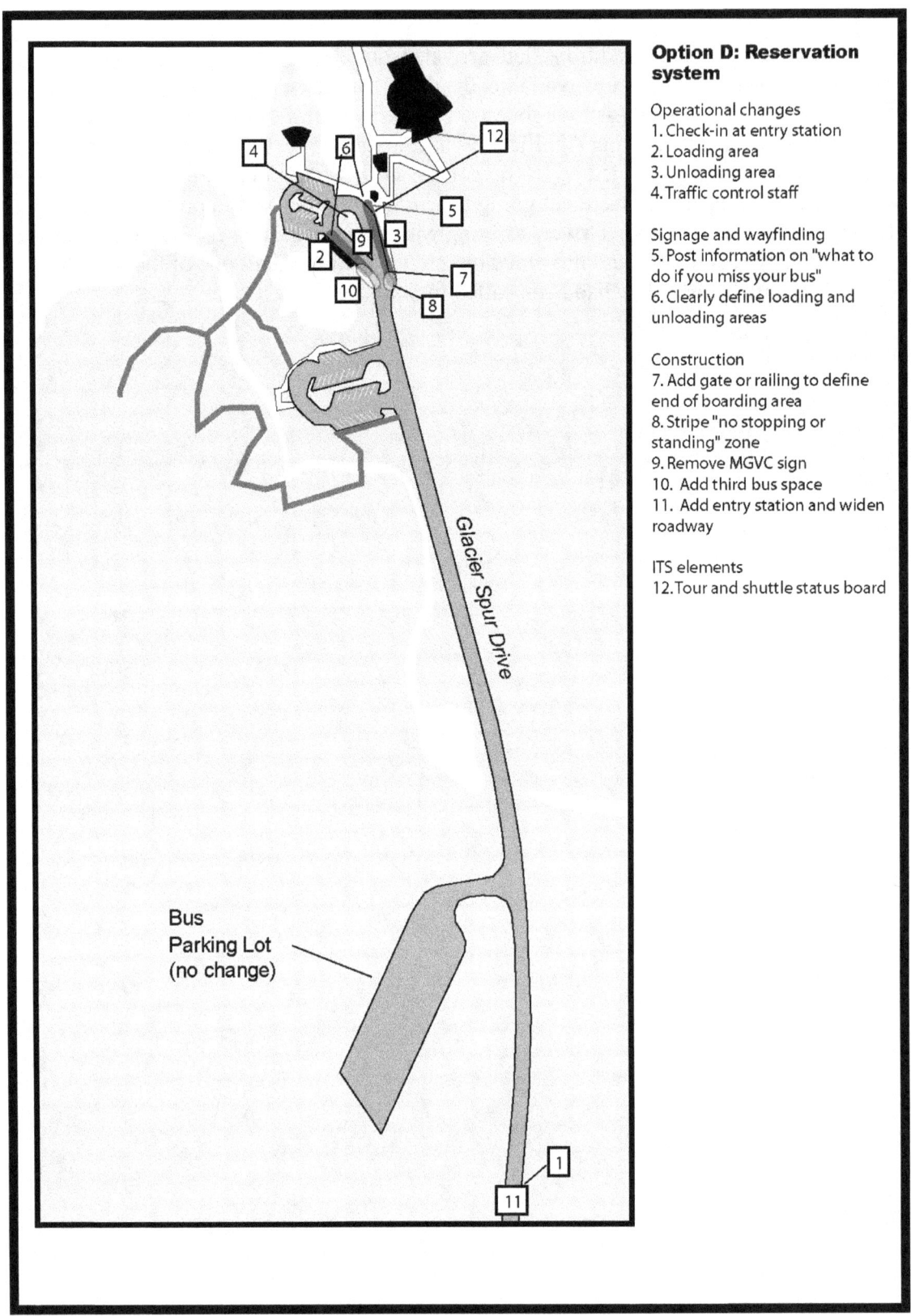

Option D: Reservation system

Operational changes
1. Check-in at entry station
2. Loading area
3. Unloading area
4. Traffic control staff

Signage and wayfinding
5. Post information on "what to do if you miss your bus"
6. Clearly define loading and unloading areas

Construction
7. Add gate or railing to define end of boarding area
8. Stripe "no stopping or standing" zone
9. Remove MGVC sign
10. Add third bus space
11. Add entry station and widen roadway

ITS elements
12. Tour and shuttle status board

Glacier Spur Drive

Bus
Parking Lot
(no change)

Figure 25: Option D: ReservationSystem.

Evaluation

A reservation system would reduce peak-period congestion by spreading out arrivals and departures more evenly over the course of the day. It would also give the Forest Service precise control over arrivals and departures. Vehicular and pedestrian congestion would be reduced. Compared with existing conditions and the other options, the visitor experience would be significantly better: visitors would experience little or no delay on drop-off or pick-up and would be oriented immediately on drop-off, and accessibility would be improved.

Costs could include staff time, materials, or software development, depending on the implementation method chosen. The volumes in question suggest that a wholly automated or semiautomated system would be necessary.

Requiring advance notice may have a disproportionate impact on operators not affiliated with particular cruise lines, as these companies sell many of their tickets on a walk-up basis and have less advance information than their competitors. There is a possibility that operators would find the system onerous or that it would limit the number of tours they could feasibly schedule. In this case, the overall number of visitors might decline, reducing accessibility to the Glacier. However, the quality of the experience for visitors who did come would be significantly improved. The carrying capacity of the Visitor Center complex was estimated at a total of 856 persons at one time, 416 of whom could be accommodated inside the Visitor Center itself. This system brings visitation in line with facility capacity and reduces congestion inside the Visitor Center. If visitation drops, renovation and expansion of facilities might be indicated so that more time slots could be made available.

Any delays in schedule due to a late-arriving ship could create serious vehicular and pedestrian congestion. However, this would be infrequent, and congestion would still be improved from 2006 levels as staff would be able to direct traffic and maximize efficiency.

This alternative requires a significant upfront investment in scheduling software. If operators were unable to meet their schedules the scheme would not succeed. Operators must be brought into the planning as early as possible to fully assess this risk and mitigate it.

Pros:
- Improves operation of loading and unloading areas.
- Reduces potential for pedestrian-vehicle conflicts.
- Provides more logical and convenient pedestrian flows.
- Relieves pressure from shuttle area and ensures accessibility of Lot 1.
- Breaks up flow of visitors into Visitor Center.
- Reduces visual clutter around teardrop.
- Improves wayfinding.
- Reduces bus idling and engine restarting.

- Achieves net gain in private vehicle parking (restores four or five spaces in Lot 2).
- Achieves major reduction in overall vehicle waiting/queuing time.
- Allows Forest Service to schedule staff at peak times.

Cons:
- Complexity of software development.
- Possibility that overall number of visitors may decline.
- Possibility of strong negative reaction from tour operators.
- Possibility that operators will be unable to meet their schedules.
- Continued mix of tour and shuttle traffic.
- Accommodation for only six active buses.
- Disproportionate impact on shuttle operators.
- Construction of additional bus pick-up space may have negative impact on kettle pond, soil, or other natural resources.

Implementation:
- Costs of hiring, training, and maintaining additional seasonal staff members; construction of additional bus pick-up space and new entry kiosk; roadway widening; development of online reservation system; posting of new signage; and acquisition of two-way communications.
- Requires meeting with tour- and shuttle-bus operators early and often.
- Lead time of one to two years.

10.1.5. Option E: Lot 2

The final alternative would direct all bus activity to the second parking lot, eliminating bus traffic (and associated noise, air pollution, and congestion) from the Glacier viewing area. Private vehicles would still be able to access the first parking lot, and parking for private vehicles would be expanded into the current teardrop area.

Redirecting all bus traffic to the second parking lot would allow most visitors to walk between the bus drop-off/pick-up area and the Glacier via either Steep Creek Trail or an improved sidewalk path along Glacier Spur Road. Mobility-impaired visitors (and others who prefer not to walk) would have direct access to the Visitor Center via a USFS-provided "tram." The tram would provide limited weather protection by having a roof structure but open-sided windows. The short-distance tram route would allow continuous operation with very short wait times for visitor transfers between the buses and the tram. To reach the Visitor Center and the Glacier viewing area, tour-bus visitors would now be distributed across three alternative path options: Steep Creek Trail, the access road sidewalk, and the tram.

The tram strikes a good balance between offering relatively high passenger capacity (for example, during adverse weather when the number of visitors likely to walk is lower) and keeping a low profile in terms of visual and environmental impacts. It can also be used as an interpretive tool. Capacity is unlikely to be a problem since the tram would be articulated, with up to three additional trailing units (for a total of four units, including the power unit) during peak visitor demand. The tram could therefore handle the bunched arrival of up to three large buses at a time, assuming that a fraction of visitors off-loaded from buses would use the two pedestrian path options (Steep Creek Trail and the access road sidewalk path). The tram's short cycle time of roughly every 12 minutes would mean that, at worst, some visitors would have a short wait until the next run to the Visitor Center and the Glacier viewing area if they chose not to walk.

In addition to widening the narrow staircase at the end of Steep Creek Trail and improving accessibility, the sidewalk system between the second parking lot and the Visitor Center would be widened. A wayfinding system to direct visitors from the second parking lot toward the trail and the Visitor Center would be required to facilitate good usage of the pedestrian path system.

At the second parking lot, where both drop-offs and pick-ups would be concentrated, satellite facilities such as the bookstore and restrooms could ultimately be added to reduce congestion in the Visitor Center and concurrently provide amenities at the remote drop-off and pick-up site. This would also alleviate visitors' perception of an onerous wait time until their buses arrived.

To accommodate the USFS tram operation, removal of some RV parking spaces in the second parking lot would be required. Current RV spaces are not fully utilized to existing capacity, so some removal is possible without substantial impact on RV users. Overflow RV parking would be provided in Lot 3 so that there would be no net loss of spaces. An on-demand van shuttle would run to and from the overflow facility when it was in use. This would provide access to the Visitor Center and the Glacier viewing area for visitors in RVs who must park at the overflow facility.

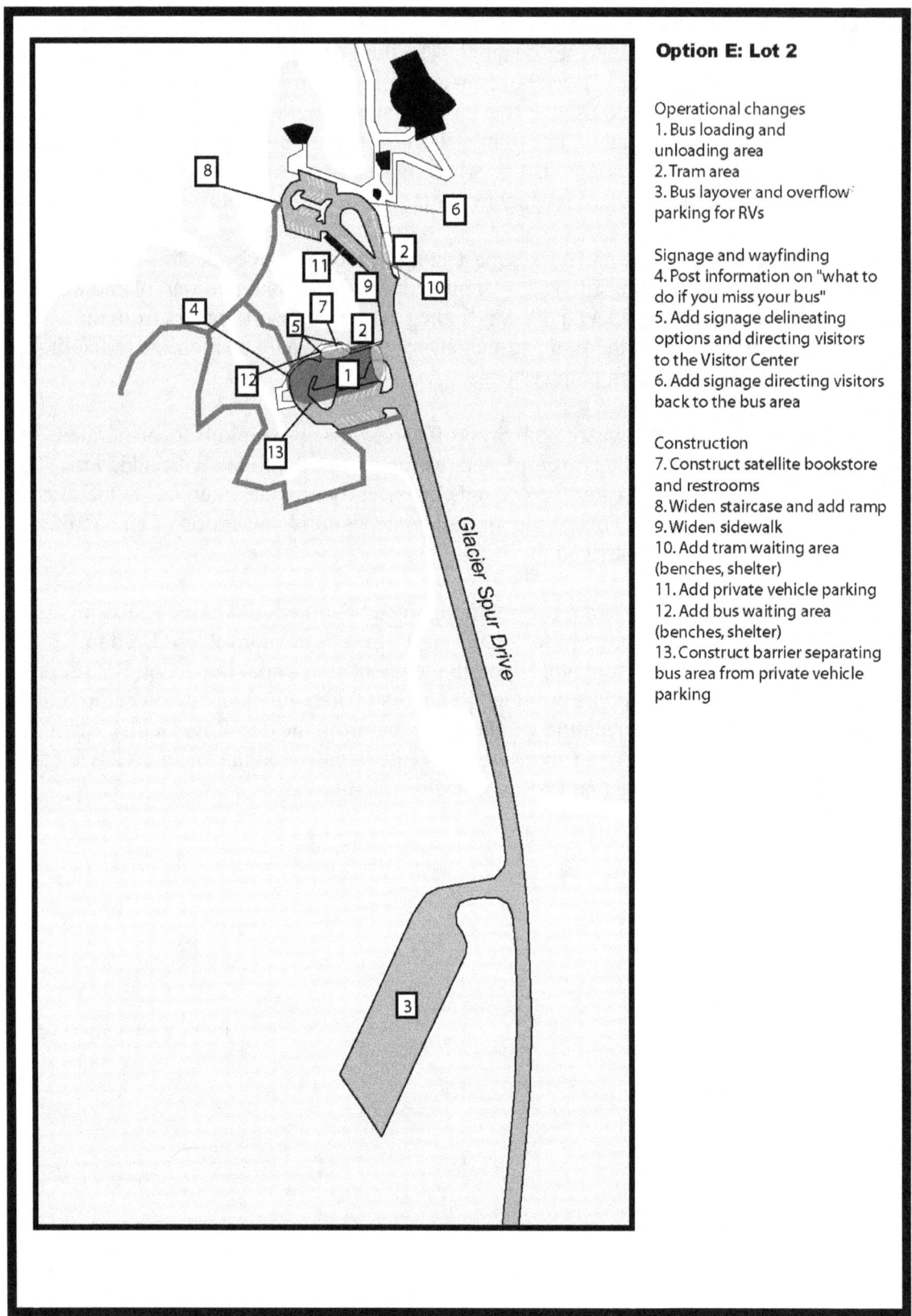

Option E: Lot 2

Operational changes
1. Bus loading and unloading area
2. Tram area
3. Bus layover and overflow parking for RVs

Signage and wayfinding
4. Post information on "what to do if you miss your bus"
5. Add signage delineating options and directing visitors to the Visitor Center
6. Add signage directing visitors back to the bus area

Construction
7. Construct satellite bookstore and restrooms
8. Widen staircase and add ramp
9. Widen sidewalk
10. Add tram waiting area (benches, shelter)
11. Add private vehicle parking
12. Add bus waiting area (benches, shelter)
13. Construct barrier separating bus area from private vehicle parking

Figure 26: Option E: Lot 2.

Evaluation

This alternative would improve the viewshed to the Glacier, reduce noise and emissions in an area with a high visitor concentration, decrease vehicular congestion and blockages, improve the visitor experience in and around the Glacier and viewing areas, and eliminate pedestrian-bus conflicts. Scarce curbside space would be organized and rationalized for "Big 3," shuttle, independent-tour, and USFS tram operations. Large vehicles including RVs would be kept out of the immediate Glacier viewing area, but there would be convenient, feasible access options for visitors arriving in these vehicles.

This alternative would improve clarity for visitors since drop-off and pick-up would be co-located. A separate, continuous pedestrian path system, including expanded walkways at Steep Creek and construction of a continuous sidewalk path with adequate width along the access road, is proposed as a major component of this concept, providing additional safety to visitors. Since pedestrians tend to travel at slightly different rates, this approach would also have the effect of metering the flow of visitors to the Visitor Center and Glacier viewing area, providing mild relief from crowding within the building and improving the overall visitor experience and level of service.

While some private vehicle parking would be lost in Lot 2, new spaces would be created in what is now the teardrop. There would be a net loss in car parking during the visitor season, but from October to April, when fireside chats and other community events are held at the Glacier, there would be more car parking and it would be more conveniently located.

Pros:
- Reduces visual clutter around teardrop.
- Reduces potential for pedestrian-vehicle conflicts.
- Improves clarity for visitors since drop-off and pick-up are co-located.
- Improves accessibility for those with mobility limitations.
- Relieves pressure from shuttle area and ensures accessibility of Lot 1.
- Reduces bus idling, engine restarting, vehicle miles traveled, and emissions.
- Allows for additional close-in private vehicle parking during off-season.

Cons:
- Complexity and cost of managing and/or operating new tram service and on-demand van shuttle service.
- Capital cost for Steep Creek Trail work, construction of access road sidewalk path, and new wayfinding signage system.
- Only moderate reduction in overall vehicle waiting/queuing time.
- Net loss in private vehicle parking during season.

Implementation:
- Lead time of two to five years.
- Additional planning for tram service and on-demand van shuttle service, and design work needed to implement.

- Costs of hiring, training, and maintaining additional seasonal staff members; implementing minor construction; capital, labor, and maintenance of tram system; and designing, creating, and installing directional signage.

10.1.6. Comparison of short-term strategies

The short-term alternatives are compared on a range of attributes in Table 4. In general, Option D: Reservation System is deemed the most effective in alleviating vehicular and pedestrian congestion. However, its relatively high cost, complexity of implementation, and long lead time make it less appealing. This strategy is also riskier as it may be less acceptable to tour-bus operators.

No matter which option is selected, safety and wayfinding improvements must be made before the opening of the 2007 season. These include clearly defining loading and unloading areas and passenger waiting areas, instituting operational changes so that drivers load and unload only at designated spaces, and adding signage to orient visitors to the site. Long-term management planning should address the issue of carrying capacity and the need for comprehensive site redesign.

Table 4: Effectiveness evaluation

Lowest rating ● Highest rating ●●●●	Vehicular Congestion	Visitor Center Congestion	Visitor Experience	Safety
Option A: No Action	●	●	●	●
Option B: 2006+	●●	●	●●	●●
Option C: Interceptor Lot	●●	●●●●	●	●●●●
Option D: Reservation System	●●●●	●●●●	●●●●	●●●●
Option E: Lot 2	●●	●	●●	●●

High-level operational and implementation characteristics are summarized in Table 5. When comparing the maximum number of buses per hour, it is useful to remember the carrying capacity of 416 people within the Visitor Center itself, as established in the 1996 FEIS: 856 PAOT. Also note that the table refers only to visitors arriving on commercial transportation; those arriving by other modes are not included.

Table 5: Summary of operational and implementation characteristics*

Option	Maximum No. of Buses/Hour[9]	Maximum No. of Passengers/ Hour[10]	Requires Additional Circulation System?	Hire Staff?	Change Traffic Flow?	Lead Time	Complexity	Cost
Option A: No Action			No	No.	N/A	N/A	N/A	N/A
Option B: 2006+	15 tour buses/ 10 shuttles	731	No	Yes	No	Minimal	Low	Low
Option C: Interceptor Lot	15	529	No	Yes	Yes	0-1 yrs.	Medium	Medi um
Option D: Reservation System	12	423	No	Yes	Yes	1-2 yrs.	High	High
Option E: Lot 2	40		Yes	Yes	Yes	2-5 yrs.	Medium	Very high

*N/A = not applicable.

---

[9] Maximum number of buses that the scheme is designed to accommodate. Without management, actual numbers may be higher and congestion will ensue.
[10] Assumes a weighted median of 35 passengers per vehicle (for schemes that do not distinguish between tour-bus and shuttle operations), or 37 passengers per tour bus and 17 per shuttle bus.

Option	Vehicular Congestion	Pedestrian Congestion: Facilities	Pedestrian Congestion: Sidewalks	Viewshed	Steep Creek Trail	Wayfinding	Stakeholders
Option A: No Action	Better than in past seasons but long queues at pick-up during peak times	Significant at peak times and in adverse weather	Significant at peak times	Negatively impacted by bus activity	Congestion at trailheads	Poor	Bus operators relatively pleased with congestion improvements
Option B: 2006+	Moderate improvement	No change	Minor improvement	No change	Some alleviation of congestion at first parking-lot trailhead	Moderate improvement (still dependent on signage; not intuitive)	New guidelines may inconvenience bus drivers but wayfinding improvements should reduce late arrivals and help them stay on schedule
Option C: Interceptor Lot	Major improvement at teardrop; delay added at interceptor lot	Improved: bus flows can be metered to regulate as appropriate; teardrop capacity limits crowding	Improved: less traffic between Lot 2 and teardrop; boarding areas clarified	Slightly improved; bus activity better regulated but remains at teardrop	Usage drops drastically	Greatly improved: visitors can proceed intuitively from drop-off and have sufficient time to identify pick-up area	More complex operations will inconvenience operators, particularly shuttle operators; reliability gains may offset
Option D: Reservation System	Congestion alleviated at all points except in the case of a late ship arrival	Improved: bus flows can be metered to regulate as appropriate; teardrop capacity limits crowding	Improved: less traffic between Lot 2 and teardrop; boarding areas clarified	Slightly improved; bus activity better regulated but remains at teardrop	Usage drops drastically	Greatly improved: visitors can proceed intuitively from drop-off and have sufficient time to identify pick-up area	More complex operations will inconvenience operators, particularly shuttle operators; reliability gains may offset
Option E: Lot 2	Moderate improvement	No change	Improved due to relocation of bus activity and sidewalk improvements	Bus activity removed from teardrop; Glacier views improved	Usage increases	Moderate improvement (still dependent on signage; not intuitive)	Little impact on bus operators

Table 6: Summary of impacts

10.2 Long-term concepts for further study

The alternatives described above have been identified as feasible approaches that could be implemented within the next few years to achieve some measure of congestion relief and improvement to the visitor experience. Although there are different options in terms of staff requirements and changes to the roadway layouts, all of the alternatives are necessarily based on the assumption that, in the short-to-medium term, the basic management structure and policies of MGVC will remain in place, visitation levels will continue to grow in line with existing trends, and the basic "footprint" of the built-up area will remain largely unchanged.

Over the longer term, some of these characteristics may change, particularly if a comprehensive planning process is undertaken to examine fundamental questions about the carrying capacity of the site, areas to be accessed by visitors, types of uses permitted in each area, seasonality, relationship to the Juneau community, and management of natural resources. Such a planning process would present the opportunity to consider a number of larger-scale changes to the transportation arrangements at MGVC, some of which would represent entirely new paradigms in how visitors access the site.

Elements of a long-term planning process include identification and documentation of natural and cultural resources, consideration of environmental and regulatory resource constraints, existing facility and utility capacity and expansion potential, and determination of sociologically acceptable, manageable desired visitor experience. After the appropriate design capacity is determined, reasonable and feasible facility upgrades can be proposed, along with their appropriate supporting systems (transit, roads, trails, parking, ITS, etc.).

One possibility that should be considered during the long-term planning process is that the Juneau Access Road, were it to be built, would connect Juneau to the continental road system and open up the area to a substantially higher level of independent tourism. This would have ramifications for the overall management of the Mendenhall Glacier site, and the change in visitor travel modes (more cars and RVs) would have implications for traffic flow around the site and the allocation of parking and loading space. Likely impacts include increased demand for private vehicle parking of all kinds, including RVs.

If new facilities are planned, the transportation system will need to evolve to serve them. Transportation considerations are outlined in the three general concepts below and in the sections that follow. Once the future management direction has been set, more detailed transportation plans can be created.

10.2.1. Limit visitation

The Forest Service has done an admirable job of accommodating the rising numbers of visitors at Mendenhall Glacier while preserving the quality of the visitor experience. Most of the strategies described in this report are conceived of as additional resources and tools for striking that balance. However, both the Visitor Center and the bus activity areas are experiencing periodic episodes of overcrowding; with continued growth in visitation, there may come a point when preserving the quality of the visitor experience can be achieved only through more restrictive limits on visitation.

A starting point in this approach would be to revisit the capacity limits developed in the 1996 Mendenhall Glacier Recreation Area Management Plan Revision: Final Environmental Impact Statement (FEIS). As noted earlier, the FEIS set a cap on the total number of commercial visitors per season. The carrying capacity of the Visitor Center complex, established in the 1993 planning process for Visitor Center renovations, would also need to be revisited. Impacts on natural resources as well as on traffic congestion, noise, views, crowding, and other aspects of the visitor experience should be analyzed to determine appropriate capacities.

The total carrying capacity of the Visitor Center complex was estimated at 856 persons, 416 of whom could be accommodated inside the Visitor Center itself. Applying the FEIS commercial-use allocation of 65% to this carrying capacity,[11] the "commercial carrying capacity" is 556 persons at one time. This equates to about 14 bus arrivals per hour, assuming an average one-hour stay at the Glacier and bus loads comparable to those observed during the 2006 season.

Another approach to defining the appropriate commercial carrying capacity is to determine what constitutes the baseline visitor experience and to tailor the capacity to its limits. For example, if the Forest Service decides that all visitors should have an opportunity to view the 11-minute film, then the auditorium capacity of 104 becomes critical. Assuming four showings per hour, no more than 416 visitors should be arriving each hour, including no more than 270 from commercial vehicles (again applying the 65% allocation from the FEIS). Using this 270-person-per-time limit implies that no more than seven buses could arrive per hour.

One approach, then, would be to set and enforce a hard cap on the number of bus arrivals per hour at a level that is consistent with the carrying capacity of the Visitor Center and/or the baseline visitor experience. This is separate and distinct from the capacity of the bus transportation system itself, which currently works well with up to about nine buses per hour and could be modified through management or physical reconfiguration to accommodate as many as 18 to 30 buses per hour.

Another option is to use transportation to smooth visitation so as not to exceed the capacities of particular areas within the MGVC site. Visitors to Adams National Historical Park in Quincy, Massachusetts, for example, receive an orientation at the Visitor Center and then proceed to the various sites on trolley tours, which are scheduled with the carrying capacity in mind. Denali National Park and Preserve in Alaska is another well-known park that uses transportation as a method of crowd control.

---

[11] It should be noted that the FEIS does *not* regulate visitation at this level but only sets a cap on the visitation total for the summer season.

Once the appropriate capacity limits are set, several supporting transportation strategies could be used to enforce and maintain them. These include time-delimited tickets or passes for commercial vehicle access to the MGVC site, peak-period pricing of special-use permits, coordinated scheduling of vehicle arrivals and departures, and new forms of internal circulation that could incorporate interpretive elements.

10.2.2. Develop new facilities near the Visitor Center area

The development of new facilities near the Visitor Center area could alleviate pedestrian crowding at covered areas and create opportunities for additional interpretive experiences. This concept is based on the assumption that viewing the Glacier is integral to the baseline visitor experience and that any new facilities should be developed nearby.

New facilities could be accessed in much the same way that the area is accessed today: by a mix of private vehicles, tour buses, and shuttle buses. The existing pedestrian circulation system is currently experiencing congestion, and the siting of new facilities should be carefully done so as to reduce rather than increase pedestrian congestion and pedestrian-vehicle conflicts. Depending on the scale of the development, a supplementary internal circulation system may be required.

The spreading out of facilities increases the travel time between them, as does the development of additional attractions. Either the average length of stay would increase, which would further strain the transportation system, or not all visitors would be able to visit all facilities. This would have more of an effect on tourists, who have only one opportunity to visit the site, than on local residents, who can visit at any time.

10.2.3. Develop new visitor facilities outside of the Visitor Center area

The development of new facilities outside of the Visitor Center area could relieve vehicular and pedestrian congestion by diverting visitors to different areas. This alternative would create a variety of experiences from which visitors (and tour companies) could pick and choose. A serious question for further study is whether such a variety would be of interest to enough visitors to warrant development. Multiple access points to the Recreation Area exist today, but they are used primarily to access active recreation facilities and not for the more passive tourism experienced by cruise-ship patrons and others. Simply put, without the dramatic views of the Glacier, would cruise-ship passengers be interested in visiting? If not, the vast majority of tour-based visitors would continue to congregate at the Glacier viewing area and the Visitor Center, and the new facilities would do little to relieve congestion there.

10.2.4. Visitor experience

Sections 10.2.2 and 10.2.3 posit new visitor facilities, either the expansion of current attractions or the development of entirely new ones. In considering these scenarios, it is critical to determine what the baseline visitor experience ought to be. This decision will drive the choice of transportation infrastructure.

For example, do the experiences currently provided at the Visitor Center have to be offered at that location? Is seeing the movie a "core" visitor experience? Is trail access necessary? Essentially, the Forest Service must determine whether different experiences should be provided in different areas or if there should be dispersed activity centers to allow access to the same experiences in different locations.

The long-range planning process should take into account the following questions:
- What environmental resources need to be available (Glacier view, water, trails, wildlife)?
- What vehicular traffic impacts will there be on new or existing roads?
- What environmental impacts will there be on existing/potential trails, wildlife habitat, wetlands, etc.?
- What activities should be available?
- Will new ("satellite") facilities entail the relocation or duplication of existing resources, or will entirely new attractions be developed?

10.2.5. Facility design and transportation considerations

If the baseline visitor experience includes multiple locations, internal circulation will need strong consideration. The construction of access roads may be required. Transport could be operator-provided as it is today, operated by a concessionaire, or operated by the Forest Service.

Questions to consider
- New attractions:
  - Would each new attraction be an experience in and of itself or would multiple stops be necessary?
  - How would people get from one location to another?
  - How much time would it take? How much time would visitors have, and how much time would they wish to devote to their visit to the Glacier?
  - Would an internal circulation system be needed? If yes, how would operations work and what would the environmental impacts be? What would capital and operating costs be?
  - If buses would be used, would new access roads be needed? Would there be enough space at each site for required capacity?
- Satellite or relocated facilities:
  - Which activities would occur where?
  - How would visitors be directed to each activity center?
  - How many staff would be needed for interpretation and maintenance?

Pedestrian circulation
Most but not all visitors are mobile enough and willing to walk short distances (about one-quarter mile) to reach an attraction. Walking speeds average around 3 mph, meaning that a one-quarter-mile walk from the parking area to the attraction would take five to six minutes each way. One way to make the walking time useful would be to provide an

attraction along the way, much as Steep Creek Trail is now for visitors dropped off in the second parking lot. Having visitors walk eliminates need for "transfer" travel, which is cost- and time-inefficient.

Alternatives must be available for visitors unable to make the walk. Operators should either be allowed to drop off these visitors at each destination or the Forest Service should provide an internal form of transportation, such as an on-demand van or a small electric vehicle.

Tram or shuttle circulation
The need for the Forest Service to provide an internal transportation system such as an electric tram or a shuttle bus would be strengthened under two circumstances: first, if new attractions are developed in multiple locations that cannot accommodate motor-coach arrivals, and second, if demand for a remote private vehicle parking area increases, due, for example, to the possible construction of the Juneau Access Road area.
- Capital costs, operations and maintenance, and off-season storage facilities should all be considered.
- Internal circulation systems offer opportunities for on-board interpretation.
- Internal circulation systems allow the Forest Service to control the flow of visitors to and from sites within the Recreation Area.
- Transferring between transportation systems adds time and inconvenience to the trip.
- If transportation system capacities do not "match," visitor facilities at the transfer point will be required to minimize inconvenience and allow visitors to make good use of their wait times.

Tour-operator-provided circulation
Operator-provided transportation systems accommodate high numbers of visitors at low cost to the Forest Service; conversely, the Forest Service has less control over scheduling and operations although special permits could be modified to expand control. If new facilities are designed to be accessible by motor coach, the Forest Service will not have to design and operate an internal transportation system.

Bus-facility-design considerations
- Could the new facility be useful in the off-season? Is there unmet demand for recreational visitors?
- Pedestrian circulation should be clearly defined and separated from bus circulation to ensure safety.
- If space allows, designs that eliminate reversing and that allow vehicles to enter and exit the space independently, such as "floating" bus bays or sawtooth spaces, are preferred.
- Locating a pick-up area away from attractions means that visitors cannot enjoy the site and wait at the same time. Either visitors will "lose" time at pick-up to ensure meeting their vehicle or problems with missing passengers will increase.
- If attractions such as a bookstore or an interpretive feature were to be located in bus-facility areas, they should preferably either be "satellite" facilities or be

accessible to all patrons as otherwise visitors not arriving by tour bus would be excluded.

- Locating bus facilities outside of the teardrop area would mean that the "welcome" for the majority of visitors would *not* be a grand view of the Glacier; however, locating facilities closer to the teardrop would mar the view for all.
- Choosing a location farther away would increase the need for additional transportation between the pick-up/drop-off area and the Visitor Center, which could decrease operational capacity and increase the complexity of managing traffic.

11.0 Next Steps

- Select and implement short-term alternative.
  - Meet with tour-bus, shuttle, and taxi operators to update them on progress and hear their concerns for the 2007 season and on.
  - Apply for 2007 Alternative Transportation in Parks and Public Lands (ATPPL) program funding for minor construction and wayfinding improvements.
- Initiate long-term-management planning process.
  - Visitor sociological preference survey: to update the carrying capacity numbers, a survey is needed to measure visitor experience and perception of crowding so that the carrying capacity selected by USFS management is scientifically sound (statistically significant and defensible).
  - Visitor demographic survey.
  - Visitor Center usage study.
  - Identify potential sites for new visitor activity centers.

Appendix I: List of Interviewees

USFS Interviewees

Dom Monaco
Dale Campbell
Larry Musarra
Bill Trembly
Martha DeFreest
Gary Sonnenberg
Pete Griffin
Ron Marvin
Molly Murphy
Matt Phillips
Fran Martin
Nora Laughlin
Ken Vaughn
MGVC staff and law enforcement officer

Other Interviewees

David Hawes, Alaska Department of Transportation
Ron Swopes, city manager, City and Borough of Juneau

Dock manager, Allen Marine
Mica, Macaulay Salmon Hatchery and Visitor Center

Christa Hagan, Holland America
Alyson Campbell, Holland America
Donna Leamer, Alaska Coach Tours
Bill Hagevik, Princess Cruise Lines
Frank Rick, MGT

Informal discussion was also held with vehicle operators in the course of their duties.

Representatives from the Federal Transit Administration, National Park Service, Federal Lands Highway, and USFS Washington office provided input into alleviating congestion issues at Mendenhall Glacier in a web conference held November 13, 2006.

Comments included:

- The Forest Service should act as a convener, creating a forum for all stakeholders.
- Consider the long-term implications of creating a new circulation system. If a tram is needed, who will operate and maintain it? The cruise industry will be adverse to mixing passengers.
- Redevelopment of other facilities is a very long-term vision. Consider first a zero-to-five-year planning window and then step back and look at a 20-year window. Think about what you want to solve and when.
- Think about the cost-benefit ratio for each option.
- It is important to include projects in the Statewide Transportation Improvement Plan. Think about obtaining congestion mitigation and air-quality funds or taking advantage of ITS opportunities through state agencies.
- Create a pedestrian walkway along the east side of Glacier Spur Road to allow walkers safer access to the viewing areas and Visitor Center from the parking lots. This could likely be done without disturbing the existing cliff or rock areas. The existing arrangement does invite walkers to continue to cut across the teardrop area.
- In the long term, consider reconfiguring the interior of the Visitor Center to minimize wasted space and accommodate larger groups. Consider locating the bookstore out by the buses in the parking area.
- The site should not be damaged in any way with manmade concrete to accommodate the flux of masses that occur in spurts and for a relatively short time. Visitor-managed flow with the cruise ships could be worked out, and the cruise lines are agreeable to that possibility.
- The surrounding residential community and Juneau would be wonderful partners in supporting the protection of the site as they become involved in your process. They will have lots of input to offer to protect their turf as well, since the locals use the area daily or frequently.
- The hope is that whatever is finally adjusted or created at Mendenhall will not impact the natural environment and will improve the view of this spectacular location. The salmon and black bears are especially of interest.

Appendix II: Strategy Evaluation

Introduction

Transportation patterns to and from the Glacier are resulting in four main issues: vehicular congestion, pedestrian congestion (inside and outside), safety, and erosion of the visitor-experience quality. A wide range of approaches to these issues was developed and analyzed for applicability to the site. The approaches fall into eight main categories, as discussed below. In each category, multiple strategies for achieving the goals were created and analyzed. One approach might be to change the entire transportation system by creating new access modes from Juneau to the Recreation Area (number 6). A strategy that was considered was the creation of a new fixed-guideway transit system. However, this strategy is expensive, requires many years to implement, and fundamentally solves the wrong problem, as congestion is not experienced en route but rather at the terminus. Consequently, this strategy was not brought forward as an alternative.

The results of the strategy analysis were used to create the short- and long-term alternatives that appear in Section 10. A brief summary of findings appears in Section 9 as well. While not all of the strategies were incorporated into alternatives, they may be of use as long-term planning proceeds. If facilities are to be redesigned or newly constructed or if the urban or transportation contexts change, different approaches may be preferred.

1. Increase space for bus operations.

The facility was designed to accommodate five buses actively loading and unloading: three dropping off passengers and two picking them up. This capacity has been routinely exceeded since the late 1990s, leading to the 2006 operation, which officially accommodates nine buses actively loading and unloading and in practice has accommodated 11 or 12. The space is inequitably distributed, with more space allocated for dropping off, which is generally faster, and less for picking up. The primary operational constraint is picking up passengers.

The Volpe team investigated reallocating existing paved areas to better accommodate bus operations and creating new paved areas to augment them. Basic configurations include:
- Parallel curbside parking (45-50-foot spaces; dependent pull-in and pull-out)
- Independent curbside parking (65-75-foot spaces)
- Head-in angled parking
- Head-in sawtooth parking
- Floating bus bays

The choice of configuration will impact operations. Flexibility is an important consideration when redesigning the Visitor Center area. Many off-season educational and social activities take place there, and any redesign should allow for different types of uses at different times.

1.1.   Reconfigure teardrop area to increase capacity.

The striping of additional spaces, particularly one or two spaces behind the three currently used for pick-up, would formalize the current use of unofficial spaces. Minor construction would be needed to allow buses a sufficient turning radius to navigate the teardrop. Ideally, the angle at which the teardrop intersects the main roadway of its western side would be reduced, thereby providing better visual access to the second space adjacent to the Lot 1 exit and possibly creating enough space to allow a third vehicle to park without blocking the exit.

Increased bus activity in this area will further increase the negative impacts of noise, visual obstruction, and emissions. It will also further complicate private vehicle access to Lot 1. Consequently, it probably makes sense for any scheme that adds *more* buses to the teardrop area to also make use of Lot 1.

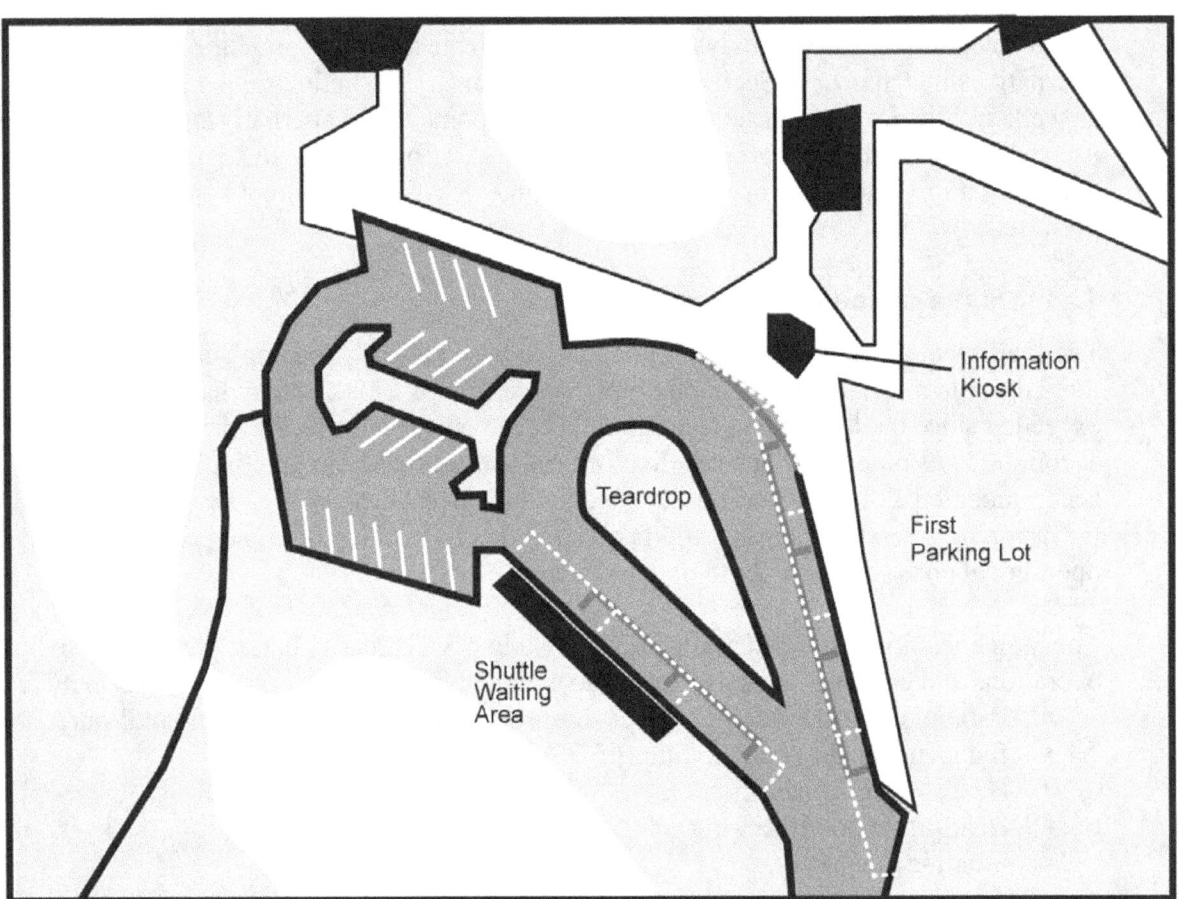

Figure II-1: Formalize existing informal use.

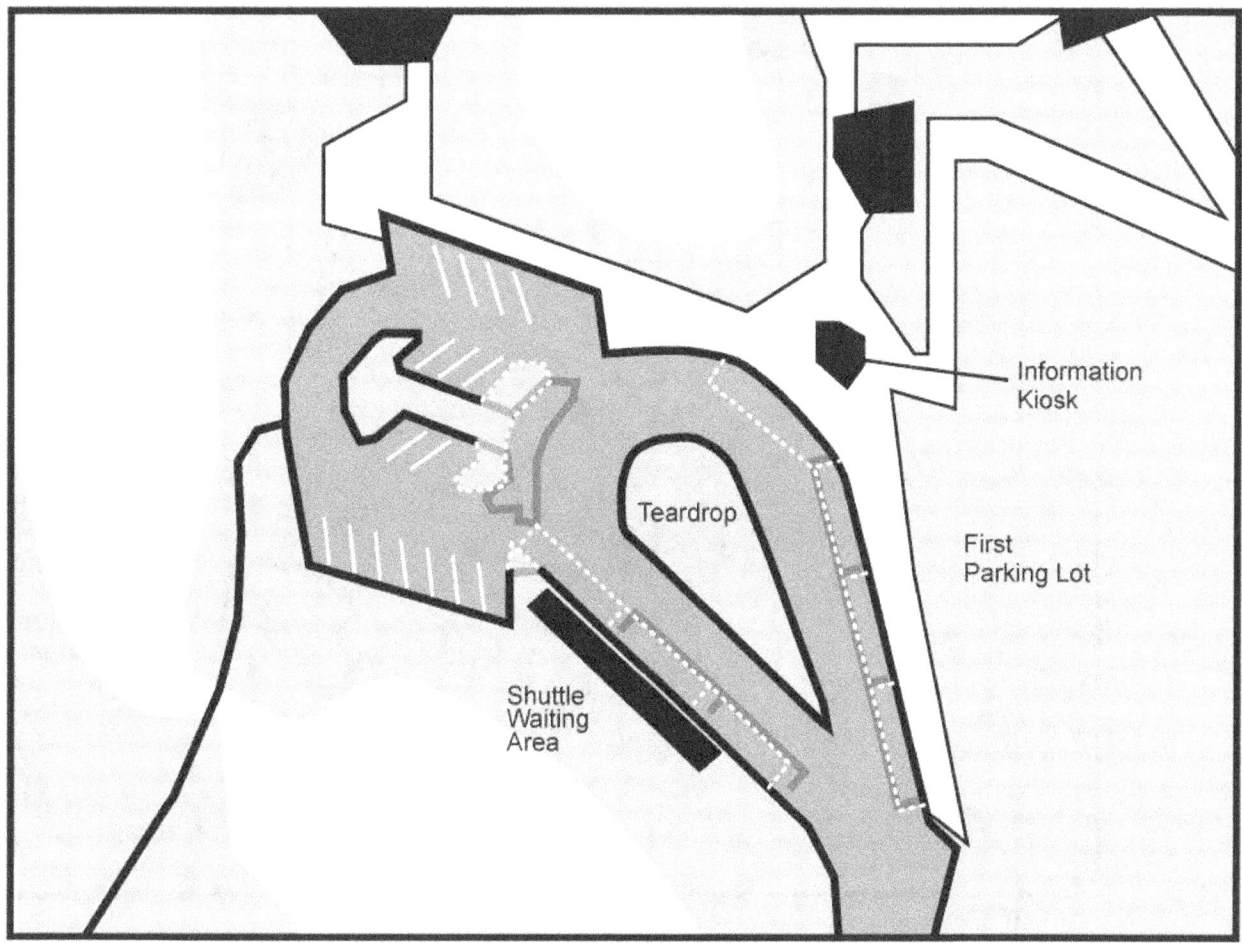

Figure II-2: Increased bus activity area and reduced Lot 1.

1.2.   Use Lot 1 for bus operations.

Combining the teardrop and Lot 1 provides room for approximately 10 buses to park along the curb: six on the Visitor Center/Glacier side and four on the Steep Creek Trail side. In order to accommodate these buses, spaces would have to be designed as tightly as they are currently without leaving room for vehicles to pull in or out independently. A sawtooth design that would allow independent vehicle movements could be used, but it would accommodate only six vehicles. Bus bays are not an option because, due to the narrowness of the site, there is not enough room to allow vehicles to turn around.

Increased bus activity in this area will further increase the negative impacts of noise, visual obstruction, and emissions. Using Lot 1 for bus operations would eliminate private vehicle parking in this area.

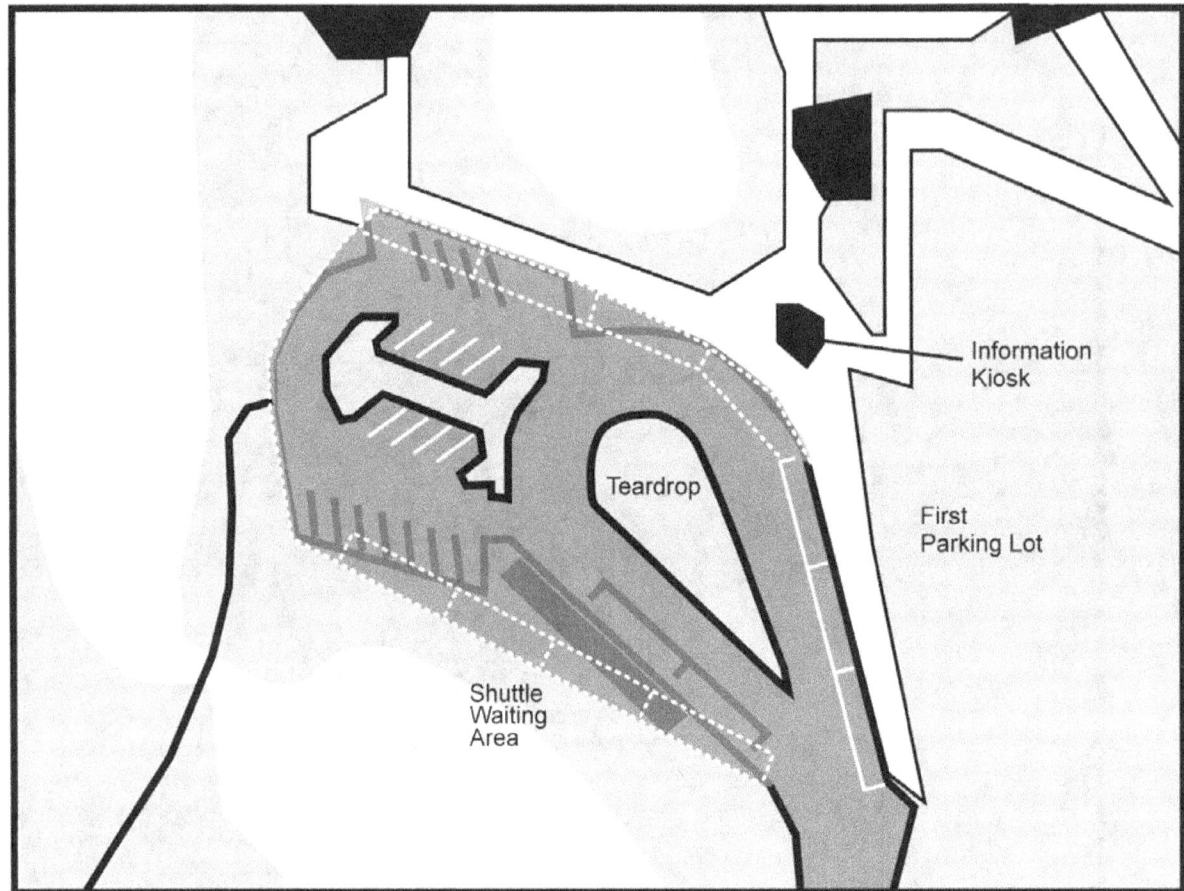

Figure II-3: Extending bus operations into Lot 1.

1.3. Use more of Lot 2 for bus operations.

The second parking lot is slightly larger than the teardrop and Lot 1 combined: 34,000 compared with 28,600 square feet (12,000 square feet in Lot 1 and 16,600 in the teardrop). Its more compact shape allows for more options in how the space is used. By maintaining the current footprint, approximately eight dependent parallel spaces could be striped along the perimeter of the lot: four along the north side, one along the back, and three along the south side. Expanding the southwest area slightly would provide enough space for two additional vehicles: one along the back and one along the southern side.

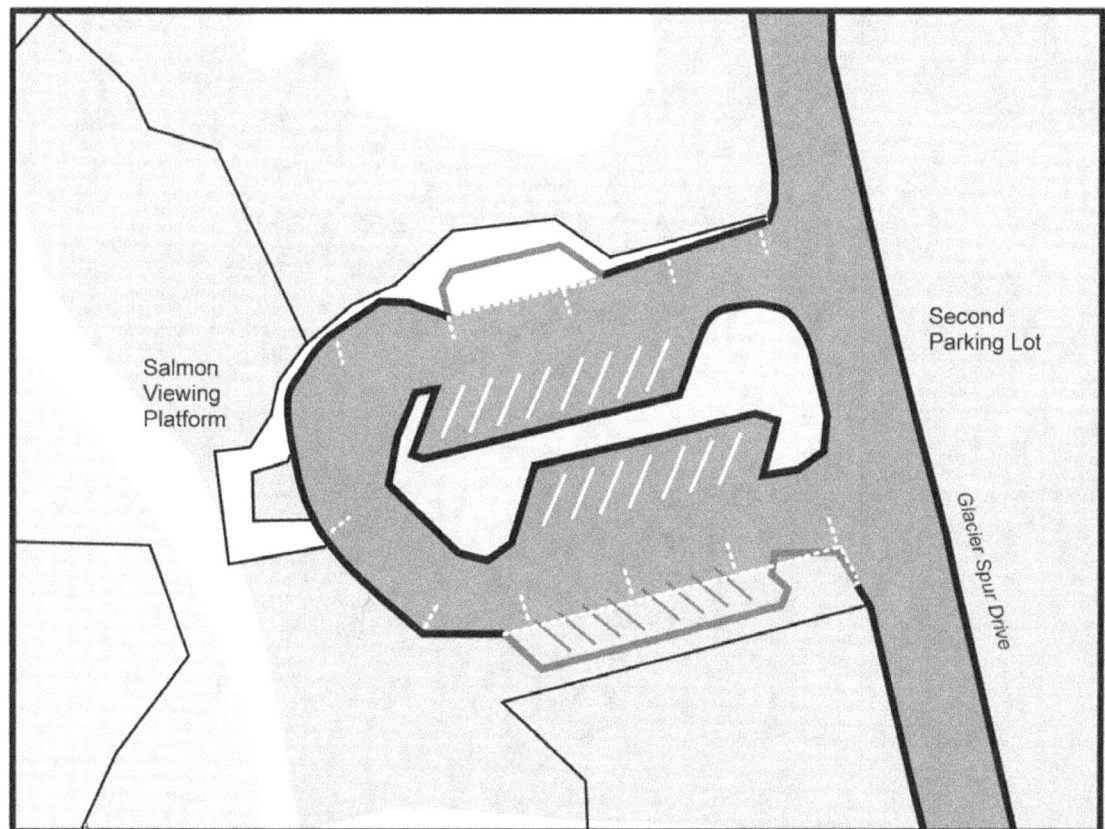

Figure II-4: Parallel parking in existing footprint

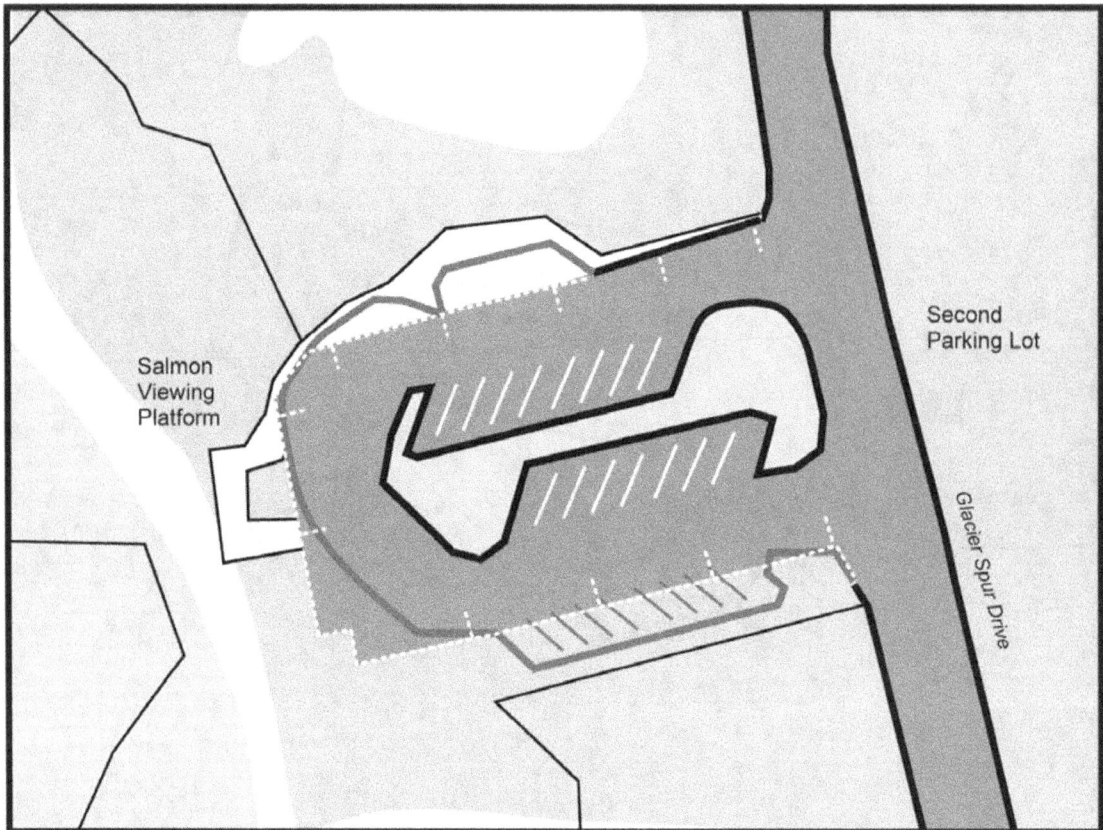

Figure II-5: Parallel parking in an expanded footprint

Since Lot 2 is wider than needed for buses to turn around, the spaces could be divided to provide bus parking separate from vehicle parking, each with its own access from the main road. Six sawtooth spaces allowing independent arrivals and departures or six to eight dependent parallel spaces could be designed along the perimeter of a long west - east parking area. Either a sawtooth or a dependent parallel design would require two-thirds of the parking lot. The remaining space would allow for 30 to 40 private vehicle spaces (not RV size).

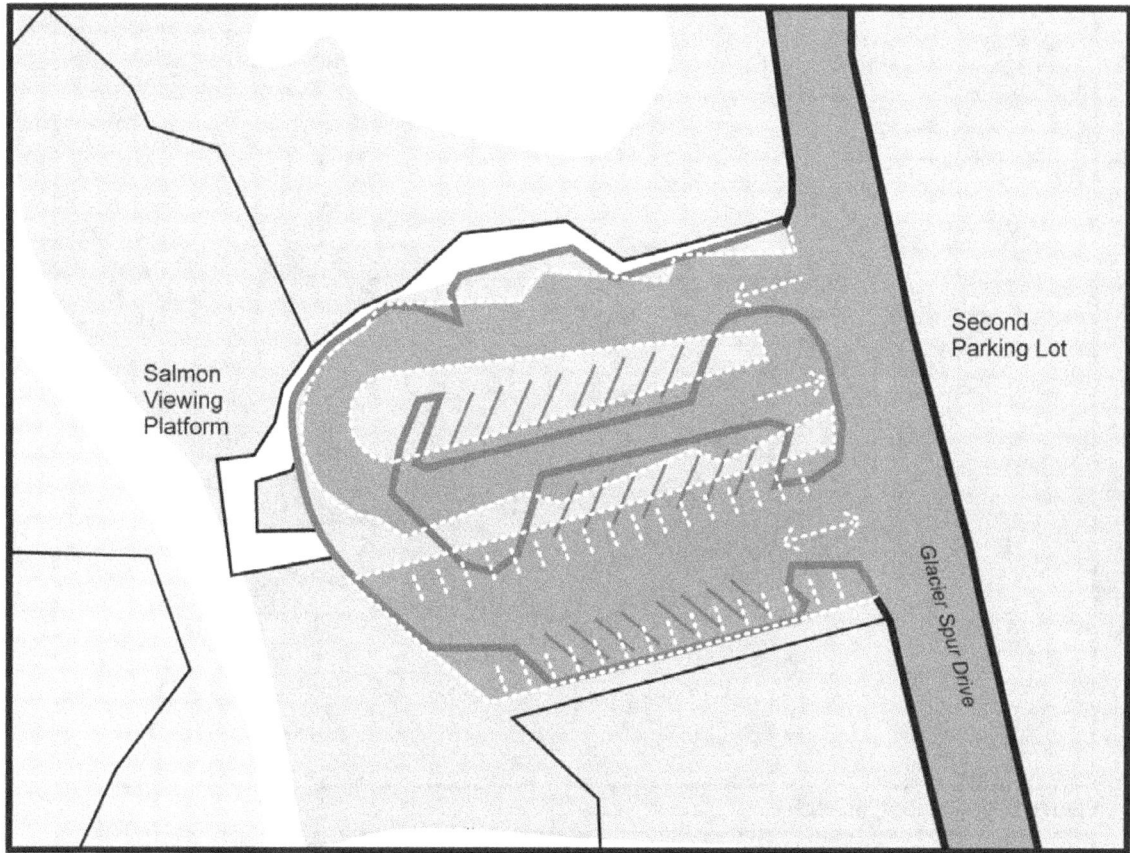

Figure II-6: Sawtooth spaces and private vehicle parking.

In all cases, some passengers would be picked up and dropped off along the southern side of the parking lot. With both the Visitor Center and Steep Creek Trail north of Lot 2, walking across the parking area might be attractive as it would provide the most direct path of travel.

Alternatively, eight or nine bus bays could be designed perpendicular to the length of the lot. Buses would enter from the south and pull into spaces designed at a 90-degree angle. Visitors would load/unload onto islands separating the bus bays. They would then cross the parking area to reach the northern sidewalk, accessing both Steep Creek Trail and the Visitor Center. While this design requires all passengers to cross the vehicle travel lane, most would be in front of the buses and easier for the driver to see. A bus-bay design allows for independent arrivals and departures, although it might be difficult for vehicles arriving from the main road to determine whether or not a vehicle was parked in the western-most bays. This design would not leave room for private vehicle parking in the second lot.

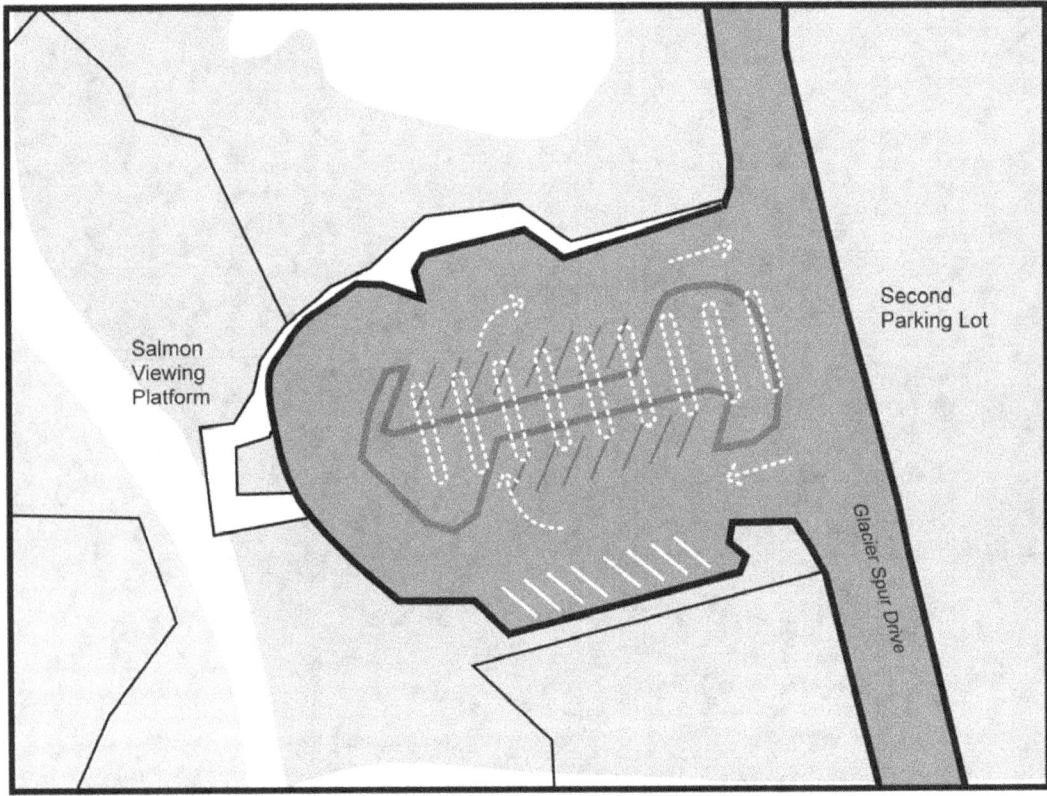

Figure II-7: Floating bus bays

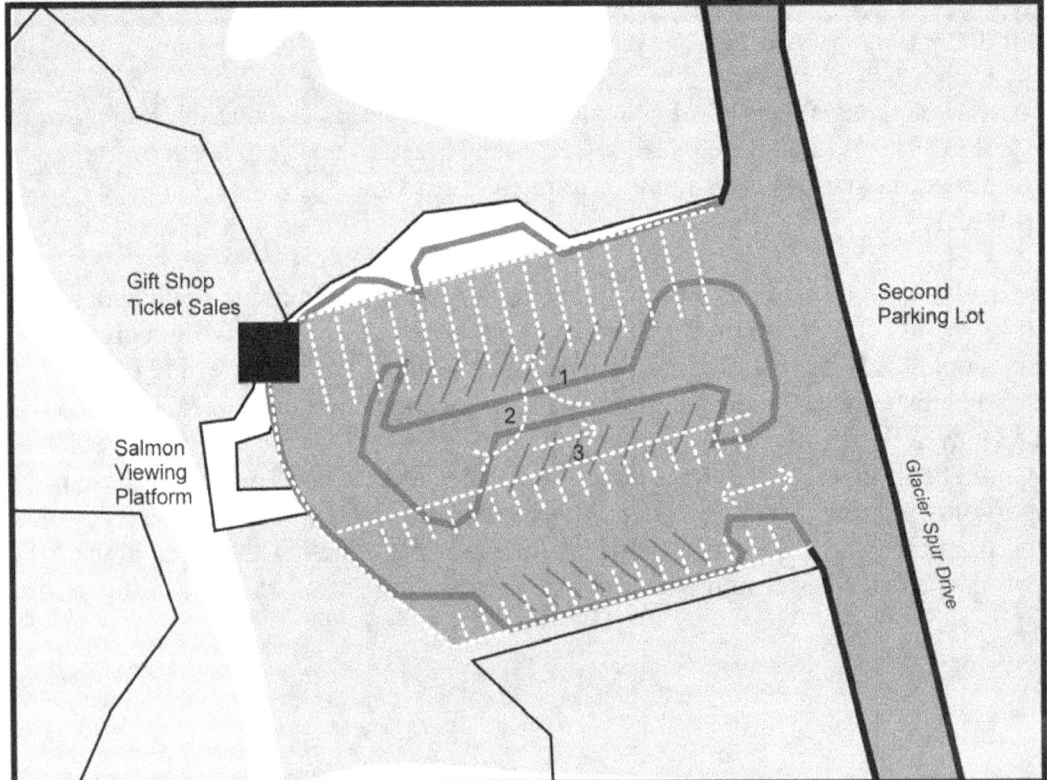

Figure II-8: Perpendicular bus parking

1.4. Expand Lot 2 and use it for bus operations.

Concentrating all bus operations in an expanded Lot 2 would provide clarity for visitors and greatly reduce the negative impacts of bus traffic on the visitor experience near the Glacier viewshed. Conversely, additional traffic in this area and along Steep Creek Trail may have a detrimental impact on the salmon or other natural resources.

This approach would require paving additional area on the south side of Lot 2 and would impact the trail systems and Steep Creek Trail. Visitor amenities and improved wayfinding and pedestrian routes would also be required.

1.5. Depress bus operations in the teardrop and Lot 1 areas and deck over walkway.

Grade separation would allow visitors to be dropped off and picked up in close proximity to the Visitor Center and viewing area but without the visual disruption of bus traffic at grade. Placing vehicles underground would also eliminate the pedestrian-vehicle conflicts around the current teardrop area and the Glacier viewshed.

This approach would require the construction of a tunnel or underpass for vehicular traffic with a decked-over pedestrian walkway above and an elevator linking the two levels. The cost and complexity would depend on factors such as soil composition. The approach has not been tested for technical feasibility.

1.6. Build a new lot for bus operations.

Building a new lot for bus operations would allow better separation of traffic. Ideally, the new area would be within a comfortable walking distance of the Visitor Center. Due to grade changes, wetlands, and other constraints, no such site of sufficient size has been identified.

2. Maximize efficiency of bus activity areas.

2.1. Enforce dwell-time limitations.

Shorter dwell times improve the efficiency of the bus areas because they allow the same space to be used by a greater number of vehicles during any given time period. For example, reducing the average boarding time from 10 to 5 minutes would allow a single loading space to accommodate 12 buses per hour rather than six. Dwell times on pick-up are particularly important: not only does boarding generally take longer than alighting but pick-ups at MGVC are often delayed by factors such as visitor confusion, bus movement, and waiting for "stragglers." Strategies to reduce dwell time generally require the presence of traffic management staff to enforce the rules.

2.1.1. Allow pick-up of complete groups only.

Some public lands with bus congestion issues, including Yosemite National Park, enforce a rule that allows for pick-up of complete groups only. In other words, a tour bus may proceed to the curbside boarding area only after *all* of its passengers have assembled there. Enforcement of this rule tends to reduce the amount of time that buses spend waiting for "stragglers," thus reducing dwell times.

Data on current operations at MGVC show that "straggler" wait time is a significant issue but not the sole or even the primary cause of congestion-related delays. Therefore, this management tool would make a fairly small (but positive) contribution toward alleviating congestion and the attendant safety and emissions issues.

The primary drawback to this approach is that it would require constant monitoring. At Yosemite, tours have both a driver and a guide, one of whom accompanies the group at all times and is responsible for assembling it. Driver/guides who do not accompany the group are the norm at Mendenhall Glacier. In practice, this means that either the Forest Service must provide traffic control staff or it must persuade (or require) the tour companies themselves to do so. Enforcing this policy would also do nothing to address congestion and safety issues at the time of drop-off, nor would it affect shuttle services for which passenger counts vary and there is no fixed "group" to assemble.

2.2. Develop management strategies that maximize use of the space.
2.2.1. Dependent vs. independent.

According to how the pick-up/drop-off space is designed, vehicle movements may depend on other vehicles' locations or may be independent of them. Consider three spaces along a curb, for example. A dependent pull-in to the second space would require that there be no bus in the third space. Similarly, a dependent pull-out from the second space would require that the first space be vacated. Spaces designed for independent pull-ins and pull-outs would allow a bus to enter or exit the second space regardless of whether the other spaces were occupied, increasing the number of vehicles that could be loaded in a given time period (bus-load rate). In general, independent vehicle movements require more space than dependent designs, with slightly less space required to pull out independently than to pull in. In a physically constrained environment, one would need to weigh the impact of the increased bus-load rate supported by independent vehicle movements against the potential for fewer spaces on the overall capacity of the pick-up/drop-off space.

2.3. Pull up mid-load.

Instead of leaving spaces open, vehicles that are actively loading may choose to stop loading, move to the first available space, and continue loading (the "move-up" method). While this allows other vehicles to begin loading, the time that it takes to stop loading and move the bus and the line of passengers to another location generally cancels out any benefit, particularly if there is no coordination and drivers have to rely on visual cues. For example, if a bus pulls into a spot and starts boarding when the preceding bus is almost done, the interval that it takes to move up into the next space can be more time-consuming and confusing for passengers than just waiting for the preceding bus to leave and pulling into its space. Active management of the spaces by monitoring how close vehicles are to finishing loading would capitalize on the benefits of the move-up method.

These generalizations hold when vehicle boarding times are consistent. A vehicle that requires significantly more time to board (generally due to missing passengers and occasionally to the need to load a wheelchair passenger) has much more of an impact on the bus load rate for the "pulse" method than for the move-up method, as subsequent vehicles can begin to load while the slower vehicle finishes boarding. For vehicles that take significantly longer to board, subsequent vehicles may finish boarding before the slower vehicle. When buses are packed tightly together, the subsequent vehicle may have to wait for the preceding vehicle before it can exit. If spaces are designed to allow independent departures (requiring more space than dependent movements but less than independent arrivals), drivers can maneuver around the slow bus, making the space available for other vehicles.

As noted earlier, spaces designed for independent pull-in and pull-out maximize the bus-load rate. If independent space design reduces the total number of spaces that can be created, active management of dependent spaces will likely compensate for the restricted movements. Once a determination is made as to the number of spaces that can be fit into the area, spaces should be made as long as possible to allow for independent pull-outs. Strict policies on the amount of time that can be spent picking up passengers and active management of the spaces (minimizing the use of move-ups except in a few instances) are the two most important tools for maximizing the bus-load rate.

Components impacting the bus-load rate, in order of most to least important, are:
- Maximize the number of spaces.
- Minimize/eliminate extra-long loading times (compensate by having the second space designed for independent pull-out).
- Use move-up movements judiciously.
- Eliminate move-up movements (may be equivalent in impact to lengthening spaces).
- Lengthen spaces to allow for independent pull-in/pull-out.

Note that both management of extra-long loading times and judicious use of move-up require active management of the loading area.

2.4. Make small design changes to improve turning radii and visibility.

The current layout is being used in a way for which it was not originally designed; consequently, turning radii and visibility are less than ideal. The visibility of the shuttle area from the queue and the turning radius of the teardrop are two issues.

2.4.1. Remove/remodel teardrop to accommodate turning tour buses.

There are two possible ways to implement this strategy. First, the teardrop could be removed or reduced in size to accommodate turning tour buses when a third shuttle bus is parked in the shuttle pick-up and drop-off area. Second, the broadest portion of the teardrop could be rebuilt with materials that could sustain tour buses driving over it. Tour buses could then complete turns when a third shuttle bus was blocking the normal path.

2.4.2. Widen exterior radius of teardrop area.

This strategy would involve widening the roadways around the teardrop, particularly the area between the teardrop and Lot 1. This would be accomplished by utilizing portions of the existing sidewalks and possibly some of Lot 1. The teardrop would be moved to retain symmetry and to allow the same roadway widths to be built on each side. Widening the road would allow buses more space to maneuver and pass each other. This would be especially important when a third bus was parked in the shuttle pick-up and drop-off area.

This strategy could be costly and may be associated with environmental concerns. Benefits would include adding more impervious surface and alleviating a primary congestion issue—that of waiting shuttle buses blocking other traffic—in the shuttle drop-off and pick-up area. On the drawback side, expanding the road by "taking" sidewalk space would add pedestrian congestion to an already busy area. It might also reduce the amount of parking in Lot 1.

2.5. Institute peak-period pricing to moderate demand.

Peak pricing, or charging a higher price during in-demand periods, is used to provide a financial incentive for users to moderate demand at those times and to shift some demand to off-peak times. The Forest Service has implemented a limited peak-pricing scheme by offering a discounted rate on the special permit fee for commercial "prepaid" visitors after 5 p.m..

In this case, scheduling decisions are relatively insensitive to price. All operators are influenced by cruise-ship schedules. The "Big 3" schedules are further designed to maximize revenues by selling passengers multiple excursions during their time in port. There is less passenger demand for late-afternoon and evening tours; passengers are more interested in eating their (prepaid) dinners and watching shows on board. Changes in pricing significant enough to impact operator behavior substantially are unlikely to be politically feasible and would not be in keeping with the goal of maintaining access to the Glacier.

2.6. Charge bus operators a special-permit fee per vehicle instead of per person.

Charging bus operators a special-permit fee per vehicle instead of per person may encourage them to make more efficient scheduling decisions. They might maximize the number of passengers per vehicle or choose to operate smaller vehicles. The latter could be encouraged by scaling the fee to vehicle size and capacity.

Maximizing the number of passengers per vehicle affects congestion by reducing the total number of vehicles required to transport the same number of passengers. Smaller vehicles have the advantage of better maneuverability in tight conditions. However, the presence of more small vehicles operating in an unconstrained area would offer little improvement over existing conditions.

Operators already have strong incentives to operate efficiently, such as fuel and labor costs, and, with the exception of shuttle buses, vehicles were observed to be relatively full already. This suggests that relatively little improvement would be seen with this strategy. However, this system could create some cost savings, as it would likely simplify Forest Service fee-collection processes.

2.7. Employ traffic management personnel.

Using on-site traffic management personnel was the practice at MGVC in prior years and is a very common technique for managing traffic congestion and addressing issues related to loading or parking. The presence of traffic control staff can make a modest contribution to congestion relief and pedestrian safety by orienting bus drivers, helping drivers reverse safely or negotiate tight spaces, enforcing vehicle regulations, and serving as a point of contact and advice for visitors. In addition to these general duties, traffic staff are nearly indispensable components of some specific strategies for managing traffic, such as the interceptor-lot concept.

Reassigning interpretive staff to traffic control duties represents an obvious mismatch in resources and capabilities. Another option is to recruit staff who would be specifically assigned to traffic control. Delaware Water Gap National Recreation Area, for example, employs four GS-5 employees to operate roadside "contact stations" that enforce vehicle restrictions and collect fees from authorized commercial vehicles. Based on their current salary and benefit levels, employing traffic control staff would cost the Forest Service approximately $18,000 per employee per season (May-September). Tour operators indicated in interviews that their special-permit fees should be used to pay for such a service.

In Juneau, Allen Marine employs traffic control staff who direct buses to park in specific locations and assist buses in backing out. They use radio communication to strategize with drivers before vehicles arrive and to provide hand signals on site.

2.8. Establish a common radio frequency.

Establishing a common radio frequency for vehicles at MGVC would allow bus companies to communicate with each other and with USFS staff more easily. This offers the potential to reduce operational conflicts, promote a more orderly flow of vehicles, and help ensure safe operation. Impacts on congestion and safety would be relatively modest but positive. This tool could be used in combination with on-site traffic management personnel (see 2.5) and the use of an interceptor lot (see 3.1).

In terms of implementation, one option would be to post signage at the entrance, instructing drivers to tune to a particular frequency to receive instructions via two-way radio. It might also be possible to use a low-power AM transmitter to provide information or instructions to drivers. Each of these options would require additional research on technical feasibility and regulatory issues as well as consultation with the tour companies. Tour operators have expressed concern over potential costs and do not feel that they should have to maintain a separate communications system that they would use exclusively at Mendenhall Glacier.

2.9. Do not allow buses to board outside of designated areas.

Due to the congestion at MGVC, it is common for buses to pick up passengers outside of the designated boarding areas. While this seems expedient, in many cases it actually reduces the efficiency of the pick-up zone and creates additional delays. At a minimum, it contributes to visitor confusion and undermines respect for other traffic management rules that MGVC has established. The two main ways of addressing this issue are physical barriers to prevent buses from stopping and boarding in unauthorized areas and use of traffic control staff to enforce boarding rules.

2.10. Improve passenger information.

The majority of visitors are "unique": they have never before been to Mendenhall Glacier. Clear, immediately understandable visual cues and systems are needed to orient them to the facility and keep them safe.

Improving passenger information can reduce confusion, thus improving the visitor experience, streamlining passenger boarding, and increasing safety by better separating traffic. Reducing visitor confusion may reduce pedestrian-vehicle conflicts and vehicular dwell times. Striping of spaces may help to reduce unauthorized use and blocking of through lanes.

2.10.1. Identify bus bays by using signage, assigning names, numbers, or colors.

One simple way of helping visitors to identify their proper boarding location is to mark each area with some unique characteristic such as a name, number, or color. This is commonly done in parking garages to help customers remember where they parked. With such a system in place, bus drivers could instruct their passengers, for example, to be ready in one hour at the "orange" pick-up spot. The main drawback of this approach is that it greatly reduces operational flexibility since buses cannot use any available space but must wait for the predesignated space to become available.

2.10.2. Require clear identification of vehicles.

Requiring commercial operators to clearly identify their vehicles is a relatively simple, low-cost measure to help visitors quickly identify the correct vehicle and reduce boarding delays caused by visitors approaching or boarding the wrong bus. Each vehicle should clearly and prominently display the company name, type of service (shuttle or tour), and a unique name or number.

2.10.3. Require tour-bus drivers to stand outside of the vehicle during boarding.

Tour-bus drivers should stand outside of the vehicle during boarding. It is critical that passengers reboard the correct vehicle, and often it is easier for them to remember their driver than the bus name and number. This policy may not be necessary for shuttle passengers, who can board any shuttle operated by the company from which they have purchased a ticket. It should be noted that current operations make this policy infeasible. In crowded conditions, many drivers pull up several times to make room for other buses in the queue as buses ahead finish boarding and depart the boarding area. Design or operational changes will be required in order to implement this policy.

2.10.4. Display dynamically updated passenger information.

Use an airport-style board (or other information display) that would let visitors check on the status of their tour and double-check their pick-up location. This would both alleviate anxiety and promote efficiency at the time of pick-up.

2.10.5. Provide visitors with written information on what do if they are left behind.

As part of the tour packets, passengers should be provided with printed information on what to do if they are accidentally left behind at the Glacier. This might include a dispatcher's phone number and information on transportation options for returning to downtown Juneau. It also might alleviate some of the anxiety that visitors experience about the possibility of missing their bus or even the rest of their cruise. The primary benefit would be in the visitor experience and peace of mind rather than on congestion. It might also make a small contribution toward reducing crowding at pick-up points and allowing MGVC staff to focus more on their core interpretive mission than on fielding queries about alternative transportation arrangements.

2.11. Use scheduled management.

Control of when buses arrive could alleviate many of the issues of congestion and could be integrated with other alternatives. USFS would facilitate a meeting of tour and shuttle operators to discuss the potential for operators to implement voluntary, small-scale changes to schedules that would help to reduce vehicle conflicts and congestion. Tour operators could identify times in their schedules when vehicle arrivals could be shifted slightly to avoid a rush of vehicles arriving simultaneously. Such a meeting would give operators some buy-in into the scheduling system. While voluntary implementation of controlled vehicle arrivals is unlikely, USFS can make a stringent schedule one of the requirements for permission to serve the Visitor Center. Coordination with other tourist sites would also be crucial to making such a system work. Currently, both the Fish Hatchery and Allen Marine Tours schedule and/or control when buses arrive. A related idea that has been discussed is the use of traffic-flow-simulation software to help tour operators visualize and assess the impacts of potential scheduling changes. While not essential, this could be a useful analytical tool and might be arranged through a partnership with a local university's operations research or transportation engineering department.

3. Control access to bus activity areas.

Controlling access to bus activity areas can reduce congestion in these areas and smooth the flow of arrivals to the Visitor Center complex. This should positively impact the visitor experience by reducing visual clutter, noise, and emissions as well as crowding within the covered areas. If access to loading and unloading areas is restricted, operators may react in one of several ways: by adjusting their schedules so as to arrive at less busy times, by building a possible delay into their schedules, by reducing the number of bus tours to Mendenhall Glacier, or by taking no action.

3.1. Use interceptor lot with staff or ITS to control the flow of buses to loading and unloading areas.

Interceptor lots (or staging areas) are commonly used in situations where the curbside drop-off and pick-up locations simply cannot accommodate the prevailing level of vehicular traffic. The concept is straightforward: incoming buses do not proceed straight to their ultimate drop-off point but instead are diverted to a satellite parking lot or waiting area and remain there until a curbside drop-off space becomes available. Only then do they complete their trip and allow passengers to alight. The same concept can be used to regulate passenger pick-ups in cases where buses lay over; buses are simply held at their layover location (or, if necessary, a closer staging area) until a pick-up berth becomes available.

Interceptor lots are used to manage tour-bus congestion in many downtown areas, particularly historic centers in European cities. In the U.S., a prominent example of this approach is in Atlantic City, New Jersey, where local regulations require inbound tour buses to stop at one of several designated staging areas before proceeding to the congested oceanfront casino area for drop-off. (The system provides for exceptions for resorts that have sufficient staging areas of their own, and for less congested times of year.)

The principal benefit of this strategy is that it regulates the flow of vehicles to the curbside loading areas, keeping traffic at a level that can be accommodated. To the extent that vehicle congestion and waiting still occur, they do so in areas that are farther from the resources and less likely to have a negative impact on the visitor experience.

Implementing this policy at MGVC could reduce much of the congestion along the teardrop and its approaches. There would also be modest improvements in pedestrian safety and the visitor experience to the extent that congestion is relieved. Environmental benefits might accrue if the overall level of vehicle idling could be reduced.

With the existing site layout, the gravel bus parking lot appears to be the best location for the interceptor lot. Other proposed designs offer the possibility of other locations. Regardless of the location, some means of regulating the flow of vehicles is needed. The most typical approach is to use traffic control staff with two-way radios: one at the interceptor lot and one at the drop-off/pick-up point. Intelligent transportation systems (ITS) technologies offer the possibility of a more automated system; for example, parking space sensors and/or traffic cameras could provide bus drivers with information about when the drop-off area has an available space. Whether or not ITS technologies are used, this approach requires outreach to bus drivers to inform them of the new procedures and basic directional signage to regulate vehicular movements.

Many sites with interceptor lots use the waiting time as an opportunity to provide a basic visitor orientation or some interpretive information. At MGVC, this would require either additional interpretive staff or the redeployment of existing staff to the lot. Alternatively, it could be left to the bus driver to determine how to fill this time.

3.2.   Timed tickets/reservation systems.

Operators would be required to obtain time-delimited passes for entering specific areas around MGVC, such as the drop-off and parking areas. The number of passes available for each time period would be limited to the number of vehicles that could be accommodated without undue delay and congestion. Advance-reservation systems for tour buses have been adopted in Kennebunkport, Maine, and Cape May, New Jersey.

A timed pass system would reduce peak-period congestion by spreading out arrivals and departures more evenly over the course of the day. It would also give the Forest Service precise control over arrivals and departures.

Costs could include staff time, materials, and software development, depending on the implementation method chosen. The volumes in question suggest that a wholly automated or semiautomated system would be necessary if a permit were to be required for each visit or day.

Requiring advance notice may have a disproportionate impact on operators not affiliated with particular cruise lines, as these companies sell many of their tickets on a walk-up basis and have less advance information than their competitors.

In addition, any delays in schedule due to a late-arriving ship, crowding at another venue, or local traffic congestion would create a dilemma at the Glacier: Should late arrivals be turned away or accommodated at the expense of reintroducing congestion and impacting operators who are complying? Such inflexibility would likely make this approach unpopular with operators and could reduce the accessibility of the Glacier to visitors.

3.3.   Assign spaces.

By assigning each operator one or more spaces to use in dropping off and picking up passengers, the task of managing congestion in these areas is delegated to the operators themselves. Assignments could be made on the basis of the projected number of visitors, the projected number of trips, or by "auctioning" spaces. Smaller operators whose levels of activity do not warrant an assigned space might either share a particular space or a small set of "common" spaces set aside for their companies. Operators might also prefer more flexibility than static assignment allows. Possible variations include allowing operators to negotiate among themselves to share spaces or a dynamic assignment system implemented along with a schedule coordination scheme. Guidelines for queuing should be set to prevent "spillover" congestion in areas adjacent to the loading and unloading areas.

This strategy "guarantees" that tour companies would have access to a space whenever they needed it while encouraging wise use of slots so that companies could space out their arrivals, thus reducing congestion. It would also provide clarity to visitors, letting them know where to meet their vehicle. If operators were expecting heavy traffic, they could be given the option of providing staff to manage their assigned bay and to help gather and load passengers, ensuring that they could operate as many loads as possible.

This would be a major change to current operations. The existing number of spaces cannot satisfy current levels of demand. Assigning only existing spaces may have the impact of better spacing out arrivals in the loading and unloading areas, but it is also likely to reduce the total number of visitors who can be accommodated at the site. As is true for most management strategies, operator compliance is key, as the system could quickly degrade if buses parked in the wrong spot. The assignment of spaces could be a contentious process. The cost of simply assigning the spaces is minimal, but accompanying facilities upgrades could add significant cost. In addition, the teardrop spaces do not permit independent entry and exit, which would make it harder for drivers to reach the downstream spots if the first space were in constant use.

4. Reduce vehicular speeds along Glacier Spur Road.

4.1. Use traffic-calming techniques.

Glacier Spur Road is a long, straight, flat, wide-open road with no overhanging trees, usually no on-street parking, and relatively low traffic levels. These characteristics "encourage" drivers to travel faster than the posted speed (NCHRP Report 504). A speed table, raised crossing, or other raised pavement design would be the most direct way of reducing speeds. Narrowing the roadway, increasing the curvature of the road, adding a median, and/or adding a "gateway treatment" are other potential traffic-calming techniques that appear suited to the conditions on Glacier Spur Road. Traffic-calming treatment just before the second parking lot would likely be most effective unless use of the bus lot were to be intensified, in which case design features should be used at both areas.

Physical barriers "force" or provide visual cues for vehicles to slow down. A gateway treatment would provide an entrance to the park before the Glacier is visible. However, since most drivers are familiar with the road, vehicles might continue to speed down the road until they reached the speed table or raised device. Though there have been some concerns with buses maneuvering over speed bumps, designs have been identified to minimize the jarring of passengers and to facilitate bus passage.

The cost of speed tables or other location-specific traffic-calming techniques are in the thousands to low tens of thousands of dollars. Treatments along the entire length of the road (such as realigning it) would cost roughly $15,000-$30,000 per 100 feet. Traffic-calming features may make plowing the road more difficult, though many are successfully used in areas with seasonal snowfall levels that are comparable to those in Juneau.

5. Reduce pedestrian-vehicle conflict points.

5.1. Move MGVC sign.

Removing the Mendenhall Glacier "Welcome" sign from the teardrop would eliminate the pedestrian safety issues that occur when visitors cross the road to have their picture taken by the sign. The sign could be relocated to an area where the space is more conducive to photo opportunities and there are no conflicts with motor vehicles, perhaps closer to the Visitor Center.

5.2. Clearly delineate loading and unloading areas.

Additional pavement striping would be used to better demarcate the boarding areas along the teardrop and to create a hashed "no stopping or standing" area to the rear of the last pick-up space. This would discourage buses from queuing in the area, reducing visitors' confusion and the conflicts and congestion that occur when bus passengers leave the teardrop area to attempt to board their bus farther down the road.

5.3. Design vehicle operations with pedestrian impacts in mind.

Operational and design strategies should minimize or eliminate the use of reversing by buses and provide a clear separation of uses. Differences in vehicle size and types of movements make mixed traffic more likely to produce accidents.

5.4. Step up enforcement of the ban on reversing of buses.

MGVC rules prohibit bus drivers from backing up their vehicles without assistance due to the pedestrian safety issues involved. Stricter enforcement of this regulation, potentially by dedicated traffic management staff, could help to ensure pedestrian safety in congested areas.

5.5. Build an elevated pedestrian walkway from the drop-off area to the Visitor Center.

Current practice is for buses from the "Big 3" to drop off passengers in Lot 2. There are several other concepts for moving the bus drop-off areas away from the current teardrop (see 1.1.5). In each case, pedestrian safety and accessibility could be improved by the introduction of an elevated, pedestrian-only passageway from the drop-off area to the Visitor Center, which would alleviate some of the pedestrian-vehicle conflicts that occur in the teardrop roadway. Interpretation could be added to the walkway to enhance the visitor experience. The walkway could also provide a new observation platform for visitors. However, it could have a negative impact on the visual appearance of the area. Further analysis of technical feasibility, accessibility issues, and construction costs would be required.

6. Introduce new access modes to the Recreation Area.

6.1. Institute light rail or bus rapid transit (BRT) from downtown.

This could provide visitors with a convenient public transportation option and potentially reduce the noise, exhaust, and congestion issues associated with tour buses. A rail or BRT line would make most sense as part of a larger initiative to improve transit and mobility for Juneau residents as well as visitors. Rail systems have also been discussed (for example, in Collaboration Juneau's scenario-building workshops) as a means of facilitating additional visitation to Juneau while reducing the impact of those visits on local residents.

Given the expense and expertise involved in acquiring and maintaining a rail system as well as the potential for broader public benefit, this is almost certainly a project that would need to be coordinated with the City and Borough of Juneau, Alaska DOT, and other transportation stakeholders. This collaborative process would need to address issues such as the differing priorities of visitors versus local residents, with regard, for example, to the number and placement of stops downtown and in the Mendenhall Valley.

Ultimately, the seasonal nature of demand for such a service and the very different travel patterns of visitors and residents might argue against implementing a fixed-guideway system. In addition, high-capacity transport systems run the risk of overloading existing facilities by "dumping" large numbers of visitors at one time. A new fixed-guideway system fundamentally solves the wrong problem, as congestion is not experienced en route but rather at the terminus. Unless the transportation context changes, light-rail or BRT systems would not be a cost-effective solution to the problem.

Rail systems involve significant upfront capital costs for equipment and right-of-way acquisition along with ongoing costs of operations and maintenance. BRT systems, while less expensive and more flexible, nonetheless require significant investments. In either case, planning, alignment selection, environmental reviews, and community consultation can all take years to complete.

6.2. Operate or require a consolidated shuttle service.

There are currently three main companies providing a direct shuttle service between downtown Juneau and the Visitor Center. Since each shuttle service determines its own schedule, there may be no service for 45 minutes by any company and then three vehicles may arrive within 15 minutes and add to the congestion. Shuttles typically have fewer riders per vehicle than tours. Instead of allowing multiple companies to provide a shuttle service, the Forest Service could allow them to compete for a single shuttle concession. Having one operator would smooth out the arrivals of shuttles and likely would increase the number of passengers per vehicle. Having one operator would also reduce the wait time for passengers and would simplify operations. If having only one service provider is untenable, each company could be required to maintain a consistent and distinct schedule, with one company arriving at the top of the hour and on the half hour; another, at a quarter past and a quarter to the hour; and so on.

7. Introduce new access points to the Recreation Area.

The focal point for tourists is the Visitor Center and the trails and observation areas immediately adjacent to it. Unless new facilities were to be developed, any circulation system must terminate within walking distance of the Visitor Center. Given the Visitor Center's position in between water and cliffs, the choices for a possible terminus location are fairly limited. One possibility is outlined below.

7.1. Use Powerline Trail to access Visitor Center.

In the past, the Powerline Trail accommodated vehicular access and terminated in a small parking area to the south-southwest of the Visitor Center. One possibility is to convert this trail into a roadway sufficient for vehicular access and create a parking area at this location. Although detailed plans have not been prepared, it is believed that the area would accommodate no more than two or three buses at one time. It could be used in combination with the teardrop area so that visitors were dropped off in one location and picked up in another. This would represent some improvement from the current system in that the pressure on the second parking lot and Steep Creek Trail would be alleviated, but separating drop-off and pick-up locations is confusing for visitors and thus less than ideal.

Unless the right-of-way is expanded to accommodate two-way vehicular traffic, active staff management or an ITS system would be required to regulate vehicular traffic along it.

Major construction would be required. Providing vehicle access to this area might negatively impact the Trail of Time, Powerhouse ruins, and multipurpose trail proposed by the Juneau Parks and Recreation Comprehensive Plan (chapter 8, page 10, July 28, 2006[12].

The Visitor Center would need to be reconfigured to provide a formal entrance at what is now a rear exit. Given the grade changes involved, a new elevator might be required to provide access for all visitors.

7.2. Develop satellite facilities in the Visitor Center area.

Developing new facilities in the Visitor Center area could relieve congestion at the Visitor Center itself. If such facilities were located within walking distance of the Visitor Center, accompanying improvements in the capacity of the transportation system would be required.

7.3. Develop satellite facilities in the bus parking lot

The bus lot has been discussed as a possible location for satellite facilities, likely in combination with a staging or holding area. The location is sited along an existing road, which minimizes new infrastructure needs. At almost 0.4 mile from the Visitor Center area, the distance is beyond most people's willingness to walk so vehicular transportation is necessary.

This lot was developed in a location where negative impacts to valuable resources would be minimized. Consequently, it has little attraction in and of itself, and siting new visitor facilities here would add little to the visitor experience. The value of this site is primarily in its function as part of an improved transportation system. Adding attractions at the site would extend the amount of time needed at the Recreation Area or limit what people could see.

7.4. Create a new Visitor Center outside of the Recreation Area.

A shuttle service originating from Juneau's cruise-ship docks or a single visitor contact station in downtown Juneau would allow the Forest Service to regulate the flow of visitors to the Recreation Area as well as provide additional opportunities for interpretation. The shuttle could be operated by the Forest Service or put out to bid for a single concessionaire. Operation by the Forest Service would require purchasing or

---

[12] (http://www.juneau.org/parksrec/documents/
ChapterEightDRAFTappvdbyPRACfinalupdates7-28-06.pdf).

leasing shuttle vehicles, procuring maintenance and storage facilities, hiring operators and mechanics, and procuring a site in downtown Juneau.

Tour operators would likely object to the institution of such a service as it would either replace their service or greatly complicate their scheduling practices. While it would improve the visitor experience at the Glacier itself, visitors would be less likely to be able to see other attractions in the Juneau area due to time constraints, which could negatively impact their visit and the local economy.

7.5. Revise fee-collection system.

One element of Visitor Center congestion is the concentration of activity connected with the bookstore, auditorium, information desk, and fee payment at the entrance. Forest Service staff are posted at the desk, answering questions and checking to see if visitors are wearing the wristbands that denote prepayment of the entry fee; those who have not paid are sent to the bookstore to do so. This function could be removed from the Visitor Center and relocated to an entry station constructed on Glacier Spur Road.

Only those entering the Visitor Center currently pay the entry fee, but its proceeds benefit facilities outside of the Visitor Center as well. Charging an annual fee to all visitors entering the Recreation Area via Glacier Spur Road during the season would better reflect this reality. In return for paying the fee, visitors would receive a card or sticker, which they could present at the entry station. If charging all visitors is politically infeasible, allowing an exception or discount for Juneau or Alaska residents may be possible.

8. Create new circulation systems within the Recreation Area.

A mandatory transfer from one system to another allows the Forest Service to control the visitor flow. Internal circulation systems offer possibilities for additional interpretation, such as informational graphics posted within vehicles or the use of prerecorded or live audio interpretation.

The operation of an internal circulation system requires either that a concessionaire be present or that USFS own, maintain, and operate a separate fleet of vehicles. As visitors would already be paying for a tour to reach the Recreation Area, there is a possibility that a concession would not be able to charge a fee high enough to cover operating expenses.

Transferring from one bus to another would not in itself provide any capacity benefit. In areas where space is at a premium, it would allow smaller vehicles to be used, but more trips would have to be made in order to serve the same number of visitors. The "crowd control" benefits could be realized with an interceptor lot at a lower cost, using tour operators' own vehicles.

In general, establishing a comprehensive new circulation system makes sense only if new visitor attractions are developed in areas outside of a comfortable walking distance of the bus loading and unloading areas.

Appendix III: Survey of Management Practices

Adams National Historical Park

Visitors are required to have a guided tour to see the historic houses in the park. (Anyone can walk the grounds outside.) On the guided tour, visitors are brought from the Visitor Center by trolley to the historic houses. Trolleys depart every half hour and spots are filled on a first-come first-serve basis, with one exception: the park takes reservations for groups of eight or more. In general, guided tours are limited by the capacity of the trolley and the half-hourly departures.

Denali National Park

Like Mendenhall Glacier, Denali National Park receives heavy visitation during the summer season, including a large proportion of cruise-based visitors. It also faces the issues of traffic congestion and the effects on the visitor experience and the natural environment.

Vehicle access within most of the park is strictly limited, and Denali has operated an internal bus system (either by contract or through a concession) since the 1970s. The three main options for traveling by vehicle along the main park road are:

- The Visitor Transportation System (VTS) bus, designed as an "easy on, easy off" shuttle, allowing visitors to access each part of the park.
- Private tour buses, licensed to provide narrated tours of the park.
- Buses associated with one of the "in-holding" property owners (principally a set of lodges that operate courtesy vehicles for their guests).

Denali is also served by a passenger railroad. The station is located within the park boundaries, but its operations are controlled by the railroad, and the area around the station is largely exempt from vehicle restrictions.

In rough figures, about half of Denali's visitors arrive by train; many are on an extended land excursion organized by their cruise line. Of the remaining visitors, most arrive by private tour bus, and a small number come by private vehicle.

The Wilderness Access Center (WAC), where camping and other permits are sold, serves as the hub of the VTS bus network. VTS buses leave on a regular schedule throughout the day, and timed tickets are required for the initial outbound trip though not for the return. Parking is available at the WAC for visitors with their own cars. Others rely on the courtesy transportation provided by their tour organizer, cruise line, and/or lodging. Though the VTS works well for a park of Denali's size, the idea of a vehicle transfer is less relevant to MGVC, where most visitor attractions are within walking distance.

Bus congestion at the railroad station has been a major issue. It is largely the result of the fact that passengers arrive "all at once" on each incoming train; the train's capacity is such that approximately 30 buses need to wait in the parking lot to be ready to receive them. Conditions have reportedly improved somewhat over the past nine years after a series of construction projects that expanded the capacity of the bus parking and loading areas.

At present, staff from the major cruise lines attempt to make the flow of vehicles through the station area a bit more orderly by directing traffic within the lot. These are mostly fellow drivers, not separate dispatchers or controllers, though at least one company has an employee serving as an "expediter" rather than a driver. No NPS or railroad staff are involved in traffic control.

Traffic congestion is also an issue at the WAC though with slightly less pronounced peaks in demand. The WAC has two loading areas: one is used exclusively for VTS departures while the other is shared between courtesy vehicles and VTS arrivals. The latter tends to be jammed by the many vehicles (a mix of vans, cutaways, and coaches) used by tour companies, cruise lines, and lodges to shuttle customers to and from the WAC. A study is underway to identify congestion mitigation strategies.

As mentioned above, access to the main park road is restricted. A special permit is required for any commercial vehicle entering the park beyond the railroad station. There is also a cap on the number of vehicle trips permitted per season and per day on the section of road beyond the 15-mile marker. The limit is currently 10,512 trips per season, which includes almost all vehicle movements, even those of NPS maintenance vehicles and private-property in-holders. The overall limit and the allocation among different classes of vehicles was the result of a participatory public process. Snow and ice conditions place a de facto limit on vehicle movements during much of the time outside the official season, which runs from late May to mid-September.

Notes from a review of the *Needs Assessment and Feasibility Study for a Community Transportation System, Denali National Park and Preserve*, prepared by HDR Alaska, Inc., April, 2006.

While circulation within Denali National Park is largely restricted to buses operated by a single concessionaire, a variety of shuttle buses transport visitors from hotels and activities outside of the park to the WAC, where they transfer to tour buses or the Visitor Transportation System. This study recommends creating a community transportation system to reduce confusion and congestion at the WAC.

The focus is on alternative analysis and selection, but the discussion of the existing shuttle services is relevant to tour-bus management. Analysis of the shuttle system from the visitor's perspective is critical of the multiplicity of services provided and the lack of visitor information. The visitor experience is negatively impacted by confusion concerning which bus goes where and waiting outdoors in inclement whether.

The recommended approach is to create a single shuttle-bus system with accompanying improvements in signage and visitor information. Improved public information is key to all operational alternatives suggested.

Fort McHenry National Monument and Historic Shrine

Notes from a review of the *Fort McHenry Alternative Transportation Study, Final Report*, June 2004, prepared by the Volpe National Transportation Systems Center.

Overall
The study focuses on improving congestion and safety for all users.
- Goals include mitigating traffic congestion and idling of school or tour buses, encouraging transit modes separate from bus and automobile travel (waterborne and ferry travel, for example), and linking alternative transport to the potentially revitalized/expanded Visitor Center.
- The study includes various strategies or elements, which are combined into alternatives for analysis. These elements are:
  - Surface transit
  - Water transport
  - Congestion management
  - Pedestrian/bicycle
  - Reservations/parking management
  - Travel information

Circulation within Fort McHenry is somewhat similar to that at Mendenhall Glacier in that there is a single access road ending in a circular drive. Fort McHenry also experiences seasonal tour-bus peaks in demand during "field-trip" season (March through May). However, the scale of tour-bus visitation is more limited, with impacts seen more in parking congestion than in congestion in the drop-off and pick-up areas. The concept of requiring advance reservations for tour-bus access was considered but ultimately rejected for inclusion in the alternatives that were developed.

Management strategies
Improved reservation system for bus/tour groups: Fort McHenry had relied on a voluntary, manual reservation system. An improved reservation system that would enable automatic (e-mail or web-based) scheduling, better data collection and processing, reduced reliance on a single individual, and more efficient programming of staff resources was suggested.

Require reservations for bus/tour groups (to enable bus access): Another suggestion was to require reservations for all bus groups. During peak times when all available bus parking spaces are full, buses without reservations would be denied permission to enter the park and would be directed to discharge passengers at the front gate. The authors note that "although this system would be unusual as a way of handling bus traffic, reservations systems are commonly used by water transportation services, such as that providing access to Alcatraz Island as part of Golden Gate National Recreation Area of California—if a visitor does not make a reservation for the boat in advance, it may fill up, thus denying access." Due to unspecified staff and logistical concerns, this element was not included in any alternative.

Physical design strategies
Improved bus parking: Fort McHenry experiences peak demand for tour-bus and private vehicle parking at different times. This element would increase bus parking from six angled spaces by adding ten "dual-purpose, drive-through" spaces, which could accommodate two private vehicles when not in use by buses.

Independence National Historical Park

Notes from a review of Zearfoss, C., and A. Eiss, "Development of a bus management system for Independence Mall," *ITE Journal,* vol. 72, no. 6, pp. 36-40.

- Independence National Historical Park (INHP) in Center City Philadelphia faced problems with tour-bus congestion and parking. The authors state that, at that time, little "case history" existed on how to manage tour buses in urban areas.

- A multistakeholder planning process resulted in the development of a new tour-bus drop-off and pick-up facility, about three blocks north of Independence Hall, adjacent to the National Constitution Center. Buses visiting the INHP area are required to use this facility. Curbside drop-off/pick-up was banned on nearby streets.

- The drop-off/pick-up facility has 11 angled spaces, designed for 45-foot buses. It also has passenger waiting areas, restrooms, and information screens and kiosks. Its capacity depends on the average dwell time of the buses; for example, with 10-minute dwell times, the same space could be used up to six times per hour.

- Observations of dwell time showed that unloading is slightly faster than loading. Under ideal conditions, such as when there was no waiting for "stragglers" and the bus departed immediately, measured dwell time averaged six minutes. For planning purposes, dwell time was assumed to be 10 minutes.

- Data on hourly bus arrivals showed that the 11-space capacity would be exceeded during some of the peak times. Some "auxiliary" drop-off-only locations were established nearby for periods of high demand.

- The Volpe Center was involved in testing the operational feasibility of the concept.

- The city pursued the idea of creating an off-site layover facility for buses (with amenities for drivers) about a half mile away. This facility now exists, with 40 parking spaces at a cost of $20 per day. The fee is collected at the INHP drop-off location. Use of the parking area is mandatory for buses loading and unloading in the historic district.

- As with the Volpe Center's Washington, D.C., bus study, the article states that using staggered or prescheduled arrival times would be an effective way of managing demand but that it is not practical, given the diversity of bus operations and the unpredictability of downtown traffic congestion.

- The article also suggests using outreach to charter and tour operators and to local school districts so that they are aware of bus-management procedures; it even suggests building a database of bus operations. Another important component is communication with visitors so that they know where and when to meet their bus and how to get oriented to the park.

Fort Clatsop/Lewis and Clark National and State Historical Park

Notes from a review of *Fort Clatsop Evaluation of Summer 2004 Operations*, produced by the Volpe Center in 2004.

Overall
The study focuses on use of:
- A remote park gateway and parking facility.
- A park shuttle system that allows removal of parking adjacent to the main visitor attraction.
- A visitor reservation/ticketing system.
- Regional transit to access the park.

While none of the issues at Fort Clatsop relate directly to those at Mendenhall Glacier, insight into the experiences at Fort Clatsop can benefit the development of alternatives at Mendenhall Glacier. These issues include access to facilities by tour groups, concern for limited-mobility visitors, the ability to direct visitors to "less busy" areas of the park, and visitor distribution strategies.

Management strategies
Remote gateway: Fort Clatsop developed a park gateway (Netul Landing) one mile from the main attraction. The gateway comprises transit facilities (parking, shuttle shelter, restrooms, and bus-loading area), day uses, and a river access area. Impacts include:
- Better dispersement of visitors.
- A "more peaceful ambience" around Visitor Center.
- Ranger-provided orientation; panels provide information and distraction while visitors wait. According to 77% of visitors, the information available at Netul Landing "added to the quality of their visit."

Parking area: Tour vehicles have separate access to the parking-area/drop-off location. Private vehicles pass the shuttle stop before entering the parking area, which is one-quarter mile away. This distance proved challenging for mobility-impaired visitors, including the elderly.

Shuttle system: While 63% of visitors felt that remote parking and shuttle service was preferable to having parking directly adjacent to the fort, 18% felt that adjacent parking should be used to eliminate the need for the shuttle. Some visitors, particularly local or returning visitors, had a negative impression of the shuttle; a few visitors were leaving once they discovered the shuttle system. There were many complaints related to the ticket reservation system, which are discussed below.

Tour groups felt that use of the shuttle service detracted from the visit. Problems included (1) the need to alight and board a second vehicle, (2) inadequate capacity of the shuttle for tour groups, and (3) confusion between the shuttle and other transit services.

Ticket reservation system: A ticket reservation system was implemented to try and limit the number of visitors to the park at any given time. Awareness of the system was extremely low, and those who were aware of it (particularly returning visitors) had a negative response. Development of the system required a heavy investment of resources. The system was cancelled, and visitors ended up waiting, on average, up to 15 minutes for a shuttle.

Walking path: A walking path from Netul Landing to the fort (three-quarters to one mile) was recommended to provide alternative access from the parking area. Use of a footpath was thought to be an attractive alternative for visitors not wanting to wait for the shuttle during peak periods. The path would add a "scenic walk" experience for visitors to the park.

Transit service: Public transit service to the park was expanded from one route to four. Tickets to the park could also be used as a three-day pass on the regional bus system. However, 63% of visitors had no plans to use the ticket as a bus pass, and an additional 20% did not know about that feature of the ticket. Ridership fluctuated daily but increased during the course of the summer. Stakeholders' view of ridership varied from disappointment at low utilization to optimism for the first-year service. Lower entrance fees were recommended for visitors arriving by transit to entice them to use this form of transportation rather than driving to the park.

Yosemite National Park

Regulation
Yosemite National Park issues some 250 annual permits to companies to operate commercial vehicles within it each year. Yosemite also regulates where buses can stop within the park and how many tour buses can be stopped in a single area at one time. Drivers are aware of these regulations and generally comply.

Tour-bus operations

Tour buses pay an entry fee at the entrance stations, either in cash or by using a form to enable an automatic withdrawal. Fees do not vary in response to time or crowding as the Park does not have the ability to make these adjustments.

After entering the park, most tour buses proceed to Yosemite Lodge in Yosemite Valley. At Yosemite Lodge, visitors transfer to a shuttle-bus system, which serves as a check on congestion within other areas of the park as it runs on a predictable schedule.

The loading and off-loading area was originally designed for private vehicle parking; approximately six or seven buses can park there simultaneously, often two or three vehicles deep. During the off-season, this area is used for private vehicle parking. The area is small enough that visitors can visually identify their bus.

Bus operators drop off their passengers, then proceed to a parking area where they lay over until the scheduled pick-up time. They return to the same area to pick up their passengers. Traffic control aides, hired seasonally, staff the area, directing buses and pedestrians and sending buses that are overstaying back to the parking lots. These aides are also used to park buses and cars in unstriped lots during busy times.

Drivers are allowed to remain in the loading/off-loading area during *active* loading and unloading. If traffic control aides determine that a bus is not actively loading, such as when a few members of the party are late in returning, they will direct it back to the parking area. In many cases, the tour leader will remain behind and either call the driver on a cell phone or walk back to the parking area with tardy passengers.

District of Columbia

Notes from a review of *District of Columbia Tour Bus Management Initiative: Final Report*, produced by the Volpe National Transportation Systems Center in 2003.

Overall

Most of the material is oriented toward urban issues with tour buses, either in large downtown areas such as Washington, D.C., or in smaller towns that can get overwhelmed by visitors, such as Kennebunkport.
- Dimensional information on tour buses in general: The report states that a typical motor coach is 45 feet long and that a (curbside) tour-bus parking space must be about 60 feet long in order to allow "independent entry and exit" at 5 mph without the need for parallel parking with backing maneuvers.

Management strategies

Peripheral parking areas: Remote facilities that can be used for tour-bus layovers, thus relieving parking demand in central visitor areas. This approach seems better suited to urban areas where high land values and downtown congestion make it more sensible to have buses lay over at a remote site.

- *Central parking facility*: A multilevel parking structure to accommodate demand for tour-bus parking.

- *Downtown circulator*: A shuttle system that allows visitors to leave the tour bus and visit multiple sites via another (presumably smaller and more flexible) vehicle.

- *Walking circulation*: Refers simply to encouraging visitors to travel between sites on foot.

- *Expanded loading/unloading space*: Site-specific increases in the space dedicated to tour-bus loading.

- *Pricing strategies*: Use of pricing to improve the efficiency of existing parking and loading areas. This approach could help to encourage tour-bus operators to smooth out arrivals over the course of the day, use smaller vehicles, and use alternative parking and loading areas whenever possible.

- *Advanced scheduling* and *permitting*: These strategies were listed as potentially problematic for D.C. because of legal challenges from tour groups and the sheer complexity of trying to coordinate arrivals from hundreds of different independent-tour companies, many of them on one-time visits from distant states.

- *Information systems*: One example is providing real-time parking availability information in downtown areas. This could mean a full-fledged ITS system or it could be as simple as telephone or radio contact.

- *Routing:* An issue in D.C. because of buses' use of neighborhood streets.

- *Driver facilities/layover area:* Again, an issue in D.C., where drivers must stay behind the wheel due to a lack of parking. This kind of facility would be costly.

Cape May, New Jersey

Cape May, New Jersey, requires 10-day advance notice for processing of permits. Fees range from $10 to drop off on private property to $70 to drop off and lay over at the publicly owned bus depot. (For more information, see http://www.capemaycity.com/bus_permit.htm.)

Kennebunkport, Maine

In 2002, Kennebunkport put in place a system, modeled after one in Cape May, that required tour buses to make advance reservations and pay a fee of $35 to park on public streets. The system was amended in 2003 to eliminate the fee and increase the number of buses allowed each hour.

Currently, tour buses are allowed up to 10 minutes for loading or unloading, with a maximum of four buses allowed to park simultaneously with engines off. Operators must obtain permits three days in advance. Unpermitted tour buses are allowed to park subject to space availability. The police are authorized to issue warnings, a $100 fine for a first offense, and a $250 fine for a second offense.

Appendix IV: Tourism and Travel in the Juneau Region

This section provides a brief analysis of trends in visitation to Juneau and the Mendenhall Glacier Visitor Center (MGVC). It includes projections of future visitation levels so that congestion mitigation strategies for MGVC can be designed to accommodate not just existing levels of visitation but expected future conditions.

The analysis starts from the premise that visitation to MGVC is strongly correlated with the overall level of visitation to the Juneau area, which has been growing rapidly over the past two decades. From 1990 to 2006, the number of cruise-based visitors to Juneau rose from approximately 237,000 to over 950,000 (Figure IV-1), equivalent to an average growth rate of over 9% per year. Most of this increase is due to growth in the number and size of cruise ships making calls to Juneau.

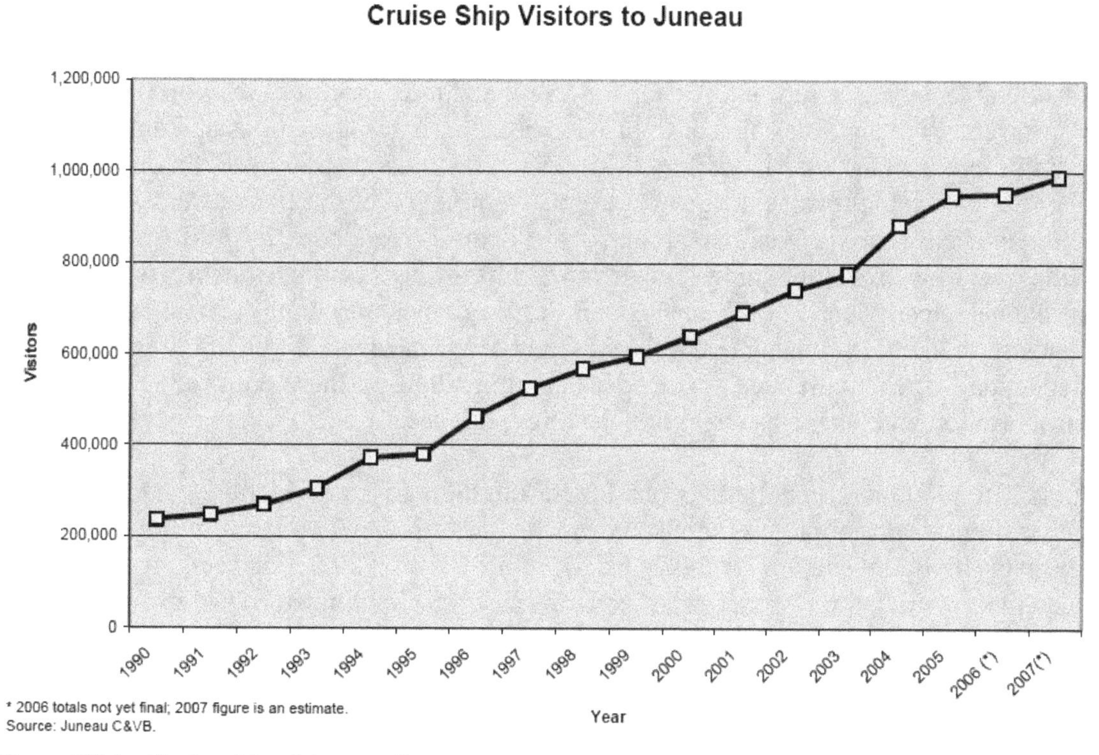

Cruise Ship Visitors to Juneau

* 2006 totals not yet final; 2007 figure is an estimate.
Source: Juneau C&VB.

Figure IV-1: Cruise-ship visitors to Juneau.

According to the Juneau Convention and Visitors Bureau (C&VB), in recent years the rapid pace of tourism growth has begun to level off. For 2006, the C&VB projected a 1% increase over 2005 levels, and for 2007 it is projecting an increase of about 4% over 2006 levels. This would bring annual cruise-based visitation to nearly 1 million in 2007. The leveling off is due mainly to the fact that cruise-ship traffic is now at nearly the maximum level that can be accommodated by the city's port infrastructure.

It is worth noting that the region also receives a substantial number of "independent" visitors who arrive by air (along with visitors from the broader region who use the

Marine Highway System). The cruise market represents around 85% of total visitors, so changes in cruise-ship visitation can serve as a reasonable proxy for changes in overall visitation. Moreover, according to the Juneau Economic Development Council, arrivals at the Juneau airport have been increasing at an annual rate of about 3%, which is of the same order of magnitude as C&VB's estimate for growth in cruise-based visits.

The likelihood of these visitation trends continuing depends on a number of factors, including changes in overall economic growth and disposable income in the U.S. and abroad; changes in the demand for travel, including perceptions of safety and security; and market conditions and business decisions in the cruise industry, particularly as they relate to vessel size and selection of destinations and itineraries. The cruise industry as a whole is also being transformed by a number of worldwide trends, including shorter cruise lengths, a wider variety of destinations, and increased demand for "small-ship" cruises.

Visitation levels also depend more directly on decisions made at the state and local levels, particularly as the impacts of tourism on local quality of life have sparked considerable debate in Juneau. A decision to expand the capacity of the port infrastructure beyond five ships or to provide new tourist-oriented sites and amenities could promote an increase in visitors, while increases in the visitor head tax or changes to other policies could reverse the growth trend. Completion of the Juneau Access Road or other connections to the continental road system could create both a significant increase in the overall level of tourism in Juneau and a shift in access mode from cruise ships to private vehicles. Mention of these possibilities is not meant to imply that any of the changes are likely to come about, only that long-term-management planning for Mendenhall Glacier will need to consider the implications of these policy changes on transportation and other aspects of the visitor experience.

Some insight on the competing visions for Juneau tourism is provided by the public-scenario-development process sponsored by the local group Collaboration Juneau. Estimates of total visitation for the year 2015 ranged from 500,000 in scenarios assuming a decline in tourism to 1.5 million in scenarios assuming continued robust growth.

Based on discussions with local stakeholders, a middle-of-the-road estimate of cruise-based visitation to Juneau might assume annual growth of 2.5% for years beyond 2007. This is significantly less than the growth experienced during the late 1990s and early 2000s but reflects the reality that expansion of the port to accommodate additional ships is unlikely in the current political climate. Figure IV-2 shows the impact of this growth rate on total visitation levels. It is worth noting that even this modest growth implies that the MGVC site will eventually exceed the seasonal capacity limit set by the 1996 FEIS.

Some stakeholders indicated that, as the number of tourist attractions in the area grows, the *share* of local visitors who actually go to Mendenhall Glacier may taper off. In recent years, however, the share appears to be holding roughly steady, with an approximate ratio of one visitor to MGVC for every 2.6 to 2.8 cruise-based visitors to Juneau. When MGVC's final visitor counts for the 2006 season become available, some additional light may be shed on this subject. For now, the visitation estimates shown in the figure assume that the current relationship between overall Juneau visitation and MGVC visitation will continue.

Current and Projected Visitation: Juneau and MGVC

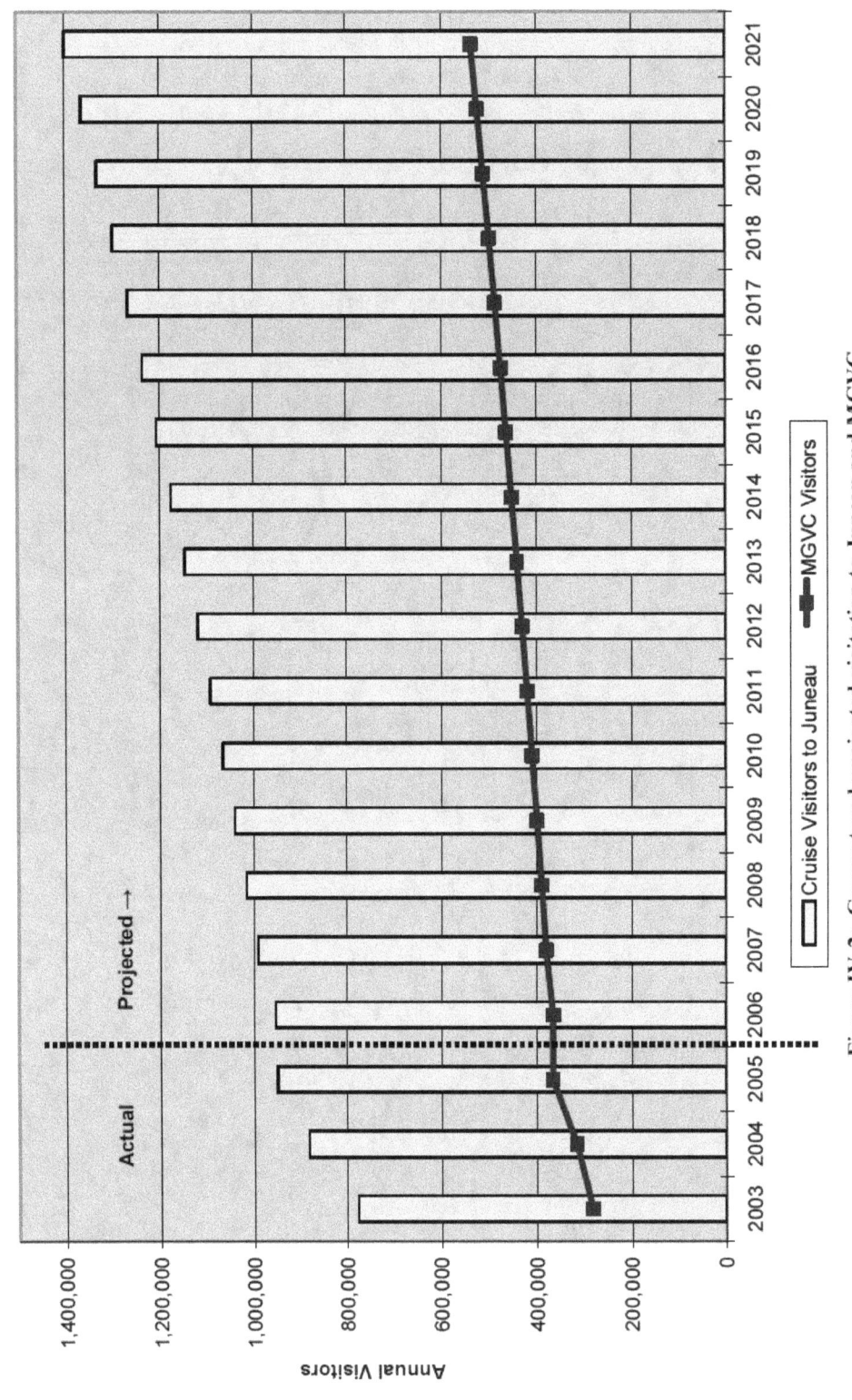

Figure IV-2: Current and projected visitation to Juneau and MGVC.

Sources

Cerveny, Lee K. *Tourism and Its Effects on Southeast Alaska Communities and Resources: Case Studies from Haines, Craig, and Hoonah, Alaska.* USDA Forest Service, Pacific Northwest Research Station, PNW-RP-566, July 2005.

City and Borough of Juneau. *Juneau Tourism Management Plan (JTMP)*, 2002.

_____. *Tourism Best Management Practices (TBMP)*, 2006.

Collaboration Juneau, Inc. (CJI). "The Juneau tourism scenarios."

_____. Stakeholder meeting minutes (SMM), various dates.

Fitzpatrick, K., et al. *NCHRP Report 504: Design Speed, Operating Speed, and Posted Speed Practices.*

Juneau Convention and Visitors Bureau (C&VB). Media Resource Center fact sheets.

Juneau Economic Development Council (JEDC). *Juneau Economic Overview*, July 2006.

U.S. Bureau of the Census, 2000.

U.S. Forest Service. City and Borough of Juneau Tourism Management (CBJTM): History and review.

_____. *Mendenhall Glacier Recreation Area Management Plan Revision: Final Environmental Impact Statement*, April 1996.

Wilbur Smith Associates. *Cades Cove Technology Assessment Report: Final Report*, August 2001.